"*Angel Magic* is a wonderfully readable and tradition of Angelic Magic, from it its 20th Century impact on the magic of the ⌄⌄⌄ Aleister Crowley."

David Allen Hulse
author of *The Key of It All* vols. I & II

The Essential Angel Book

Angel Magic is a stimulating and intriguing look at the many and varied forms of angels throughout history and the intriguing forms of magic that have sprung up around these beings. Geoffrey James skillfully and entertainingly reveals the development of angel magic and its role in Islam, Gnosticism, Christianity, Cabala, and other religious and magical traditions. *Angel Magic* goes beyond the fads and pop culture icons, providing the serious student with a wealth of insight and a firm foundation for their own explorations into the subtle realms of the angels.

Come along on a fascinating journey back in time to discover the origin of humanity's powerful and persistent belief in angels. Compiled from over 100 hard to find texts, grimoires, and rare manuscripts, *Angel Magic* is the ultimate primer for anyone interested in the mysteries of angelic magical traditions.

About the Author

Geoffrey James is an adjunct faculty member at Boston University and teaches management courses at the University of California and the University of Washington. The only son of an Episcopalian priest and a Buddhist, he received a degree in English Magna Cum Laude from the University of California at Irvine, where he was a Rhodes Scholarship candidate and elected Phi Beta Kappa. His interest in magic dates back to his college years, when he studied medieval and Renaissance literature. He has travelled worldwide, and written numerous books and articles related to the New Age. Today, he lives and works out of his hexagonal house perched on a rock-strewn hilltop in the middle of the New England woods.

To Write the Author

If you wish to contact the author or would like more information about this book, please write to the author in care of Llewellyn Worldwide, and we will forward your request. Both the author and publisher appreciate hearing from you and learning of your enjoyment of this book and how it has helped you. Llewellyn Worldwide cannot guarantee that every letter written to the author can be answered, but all will be forwarded. Please write to:

Geoffrey James
c/o Llewellyn Worldwide
P.O. Box 64383, Dept. K368-9, St. Paul, MN 55164-0383, U.S.A.
Please enclose a self-addressed, stamped envelope for reply, or $1.00 to cover costs.
If outside U.S.A., enclose international postal reply coupon.

WORLD RELIGION AND MAGIC

ANGEL MAGIC

THE ANCIENT ART OF SUMMONING AND COMMUNICATING WITH ANGELIC BEINGS

GEOFFREY JAMES

1999
Llewellyn Publications
St. Paul, Minnesota 55164-0383, U.S.A.

FIRST EDITION
Third Printing, 1999

Cover Illustration: Jonnie Curry
Cover Design: Anne Marie Garrison
Book Design and Layout: Designed To Sell

Library of Congress Cataloging-in-Publication Data
James, Geoffrey, 1942-
    Angel magic : the ancient art of summoning & communicating with angelic beings / Geoffrey James.
        p.   cm. — (World religion and magic series)
    Includes bibliographical references and index.
    ISBN 1-56718-368-9 (pbk.)
    1. Magic. 2. Angels—Miscellanea.   I. Title. II. Series:
Llewellyn's world religion & magic series.
BF1623.A53J35 1995
    133.4—dc20   95-19879
                                                                              CIP

Publisher's note:
Llewellyn Worldwide does not participate in, endorse, or have any authority or responsibility concerning private business transactions between our authors and the public.
    All mail addressed to the author is forwarded but the publisher cannot, unless specifically instructed by the author, give out an address or phone number.

Llewellyn Publications
A Division of Llewellyn Worldwide, Ltd.
P.O. Box 64383, St. Paul, MN 55164-0383

Printed in the United States of America

Llewellyn's World Religion and Magic Series

At the core of every religion, at the foundation of every culture, there is MAGIC.

Magic sees the worlds as alive, as the home which humanity shares with beings and powers both visible and invisible with whom and which we can interface to either our advantage or disadvantage—depending upon our awareness and intention.

Religious worship and communion is one kind of magic, and just as there are many religions in the world, so are there many magical systems.

Religion and magic are ways of seeing and relating to the creative powers, the living energies, the all-pervading spirit, the underlying intelligence that is the universe within which we and all else exist.

Neither religion nor magic conflicts with science. All share the same goals and the same limitations: always seeking truth, forever haunted by human limitations in perceiving that truth. Magic is "technology" based upon experience and extrasensory insight, providing its practitioners with methods of greater influence and control over the world of the invisible before it impinges on the world of the visible.

The study of magic not only enhances your understanding of the world in which you live, and hence your ability to live better, but brings you into touch with the inner essence of your long evolutionary heritage and most particularly—as in the case of the magical system identified most closely with your genetic inheritance—with the archetypal images and forces most alive in your whole consciousness.

Other Books by the Author

Enochian Evocation (Heptangle, 1984)

Document Databases (Van Nostrand Reinhold, 1985)

The Tao of Programming (InfoBooks, 1987)

The Zen of Programming (InfoBooks, 1988)

Computer Parables (InfoBooks, 1989)

The Enochian Magick of Doctor John Dee (Llewellyn, 1994)

FOR DEAR LITTLE MARIAN

Contents

List of Illustrations

List of Figures

Preface

I began this book twenty years ago when I was a student of English literature at the University of California at Irvine. One quarter I attended a course on the Elizabethan playwrights and another course on the works of William Blake. For the first course, I wrote a paper identifying the sources of the magical ceremonies in Marlowe's play Doctor Faustus. For the second, I wrote a paper suggesting that Blake practiced Angel Magic to obtain the visions he described in his poems. Neither paper was well received by the professors, who considered my ideas as being outside the traditional parameters of academia.

This only served to pique my interest, however. I continued researching the literature and history of Magic and Religion and after graduation wrote a series of articles for Gnostica magazine (a Llewellyn publication of the late 1970s). These articles traced the history of Angel Magic from its inception in ancient Chaldea, all the way to modern times. Unfortunately, the magazine ceased publication before the entire series was published. I had always intended to gather the articles — both published and unpublished — into book format, but somehow always managed to lack the time. It wasn't until 1993 that I actually got around to making a formal proposal to Llewellyn. They liked the idea, and the result is the volume that you now hold in your hands.

I'm often asked whether or not I am a "true believer" in Angel Magic. I have to confess that my interest in these matters is primarily historical. This is not to say that I'm a diehard materialist, or worse, one of those prissy scholars who poo-poo anything that doesn't fit the curriculum of a twentieth-century university. To the contrary, I consider myself open-minded and willing to take any set of phenomena on its own terms. Personally, I've seen some rather strange things that would be difficult for a strict materialist to explain away; however, I've yet to see an Angel with my waking eyes.

At this time, I'd like to thank Nancy J. Mostad of Llewellyn for encouraging me to continue writing on these subjects, Llewellyn Publisher Carl Weschcke for creating a publishing environment that fosters alternative approaches, Janine Ranee for remaining a long-distance friend through all the changes in our lives, Donald Tyson for his excellent suggestions to improve the first draft, Master Yang Jwing-Ming for always encouraging me to seek the highest levels of excellence, and Anthony J. Robbins for teaching me how to live with passion.

Geoffrey James
Maui, September 1994

The Boat of Souls

Introduction
to Angel Magic

ngel Magic is the ancient art of summoning and communicating with Angelic beings. Belief in Angel Magic is as old the belief in Angels. Throughout history, sages have claimed to have the power to call Angels down from heaven—or fallen Angels up from hell—for the purpose of learning their secrets and using their supernatural powers. This chapter discusses the nature of Angels and the basic principles of Angel Magic, through which saints and sorcerers have sought supreme enlightenment.

WHAT ARE ANGELS?

The modern world has rediscovered Angels. Glutted with the runaway materialism and greed of the 1980s, people are beginning to turn to personal growth and spiritual development. This evolution in human thought is expressing itself in a renewed interest in Angels, those mysterious semi-divine beings who figure so greatly in folk tales and religious writing throughout the world.

This fascination with Angels is not a cult phenomenon. It has a wide base of interest. A recent survey by *Time* magazine revealed that fully sixty-nine percent of Americans believe in the existence of Angels.[1]

Along with this renewed interest comes a number of questions. People may believe in Angels, but they're uncertain as to their nature and purpose. In the past, most people would have looked to priests and pastors for the answer to these questions. Today, people aren't so sure that the established church has the answers.

In fact, the belief in Angels far antedates the established Christian church. People in many cultures throughout the ages have believed in Angels. This fact suggests that either there is some deeper reality behind the belief or that the very idea provides an important benefit to the human psyche. In either case, there is something mysterious at work when people continue to believe in the existence of something that is not only very ancient but totally contrary to the principles of modern science and popular materialism.

According to Christian tradition, Angels are spiritual entities that God created before He created Adam and Eve. The Angels were appointed to rule over the stars, the planets, and the different regions of the earth. While Angels appear throughout the Bible, they remain mysterious beings of unknown power.

Part of our fascination with Angels is that they don't seem to be strictly necessary. After all, if God is omnipotent, why would he need a crowd of lesser beings to help him administer and protect the earth? Angels not only defy theology, they reach beyond logic and into the deepest desires and aspirations of the human race.

According to the legends, not all Angels are benign. In the Christian tradition, the most powerful Angel was Satan, who rebelled against God and, as a punishment, was cast into hell. A number of other Angels rebelled with him and it is these fallen Angels that make up the hordes of devils so prone to tempt mankind.

Like good Angels, the devils raise difficult theological questions. Why, for example, would God allow them to exist at all? It seems to violate all rules of common sense for the supreme being to allow the earth to be plagued by noxious spirits. The problem is made worse by passages in the Bible that seem to suggest that there's not a great deal of difference between Angels and devils anyway. In the Book of Job, for example, God and Satan seem almost like cronies, hobnobbing and wagering about the fate of the hapless Job. Clearly, both Angels and devils belong to an older tradition, one that precedes the formation of the Christian church. They appear, in different guises, in the folklore and religious tales of hundreds of cultures. What the Christians call Angels, other religions call the gods, divas, jinn, kamis, or daimones.

The Greeks, for example, believed in the existence of gods whose function was the same as Christian Angels. They watched over the heavens and controlled various aspects of the human and natural worlds. Just as Christian theology postulates a hierarchy of Angels, from the mighty Cherubim down to the lowly Archangels, the Greeks saw the spiritual world separated into the greater Gods of the heavens and the lesser gods of the woods and fields. Just as some Christians believe that each person has an individual guardian Angel, the Greeks believed that each person had a "daimon"—a guardian Angel—that represented his or her highest spiritual self.

Interestingly, the Greek word daimon is the source of the word demon. It was the Christians that equated the term daimon (demon) with the devils. The early Christians insisted that the gods and Angels of other cultures must, by definition, be devils in disguise. In this way, Ishtar, the Babylonian Angel of the moon became, in Christian demonology, the devil Astaroth. This demonization of the old gods did not take place everywhere. In the Celtic countries, the Angels of the druids were incorporated into the Christian hierarchy. For example, the Celtic goddess Brigit became, in Christian mythology, the good Saint Brigit.

The early Christians were unusual in their intolerance for the Angels of other cultures. The Greeks, the Romans and the Celts tended to accept all religions as valid ways to express respect and love for the divine power. The same kind of tolerance has always been the rule in the Orient. Hinduism, Buddhism, Shinto and Taoism treat gods, Angels and other spirits as manifestations of the divine energy that informs and empowers everything in the universe.

Unlike Christianity, oriental religions don't separate Angels into good and evil. Instead, they believe that all Angels represent divine energy, although that energy may appear as evil from the human viewpoint. The Taoist Yin-Yang symbol represents this interplay of opposing forces in the universe. To the Taoists, good and evil are sides of the same coin.

This difference in philosophical viewpoint gives us a different perspective on Angels. Oriental religion treats spiritual beings as if they were placed on a sliding scale. At one end of the scale are the highly powerful beings that have nearly reached Nirvana. At the other end are the weak but mischievous beings that play pranks and cause sickness. Regardless of their level of development, such spirits are manifestations of divine energy; however, just like human beings, these manifestations are at different points in their spiritual development.

An echo of this concept can be found in the Christian traditions of the "neutral" Angels. According to European folklore, there exist certain Angels that didn't participate in the war between God and Satan. These are the Fairies—the spirits of the woods, rivers and fields, who represent the power of nature. It is these neutral Angels who guard the

Holy Grail in the story of Percival.[2] They are a mixture of good and evil—just like human beings.

[ornament]

ARE ANGELS REAL?

The belief in Angels is a nearly universal phenomenon. The fact that the belief has remained so persistently in the human consciousness tells us that there is something deep at work. Either the human mind has a propensity to believe in things that are nonsensical or there is some higher reality underlying the belief. Modern science and psychology do an excellent job of treating mystical experiences as if they were hallucinations. It is rare that anyone dares to take a look at the possibility that Angels might actually be real.

The psychologist Carl Jung was one of the first to point out that the myths and legends of different countries have a great deal in common. He postulated the existence of a collective unconscious, a realm in the mind peopled by symbolic figures and, as he put it, "primordial types…that have existed since the remotest times." Visions of Angels are, under Jung's theory, a result of "racial memory"—a genetic propensity of the human mind to imagine the same kind of images and ideas. According to Jung, it is this racial memory that results in the presence of Angels in the religions of so many cultures, even those that were geologically isolated for thousands of years.[3]

Jung's theory, on the surface, seems to reduce Angels to mere phantasms of the mind. There is, however, a completely opposite way to interpret Jung's observations. Consider that perception is the only means by which the reality of the universe can be deduced. So-called objective reality is only a consensus of observations. We believe that a chair, for example, is real because we all can see it with our eyes and feel it with our hands. The objective reality of the chair is dependent upon the fact that everyone agrees that it actually exists. The exact same thing is true of Jung's archetypes. Angels appear in the dreams and visions of all humans, so Angels have as much objective reality as a physical object.

To see why this is true, let's imagine a fictional country where everybody is highly nearsighted. One day, a normal child is washed ashore and raised by the nearsighted natives. The normal child looks up at the sky and sees stars. "What are those?" he asks, pointing up at the sky.

"What are you talking about?" they respond, "We see nothing at all." Under these circumstances, the normal child might well conclude that the stars were only a hallucination he was having and were not actually real.

Now it happens that this nearsighted culture has a tradition of telling stories based upon dreams. They sit around a fire each night and tell about the images that appeared in their minds the night before. Each dream is filled with similar images and archetypes—the wise woman, the trickster, the warrior maiden, etc. The normal child has similar dreams and participates easily in the discussions. Under these circumstance, the child would probably conclude that the dream-archetypes, which everyone sees, were more real than the stars, which only he can see.

One day, the child is walking on the beach and sees a sailing ship. He swims out to it and is taken back to where he was born. There he notices that nearly everybody can see the stars as well as he can. "So the stars are just as real as the creatures that appear in dreams," he says happily. His new companions don't understand. "What are you talking about?" they ask, "Dreams aren't real! You can't touch them."

"But you can't touch the stars, either!" he responds angrily. From his viewpoint, his new companions may not be nearsighted, but they are certainly inconsistent about their definitions of reality. The point of this story is that it is mere prejudice to consider Angels unreal just because they don't seem to fit our preconceived notions of the nature of reality.

It could be argued that Angels aren't real because people don't see them at the same time. When two people see a chair, it looks more or less the same to each of them, and they can see it at the same time. By contrast, dreams and visions of Angels are often highly personal. A person may see an Angel that looks like something out of picture book that he or she read as a child. The Angel might appear with the face of a loved one who is no longer living. Angels also appear in different ways to people in different cultures. If Angels are real, how can they take on so many different forms?

A good way to explain this phenomenon is to consider the possibility of a sixth sense by which humans can perceive an Angelic presence. The myths and legends of hundreds of cultures reinforce the notion that certain humans are gifted with a level of sensitivity that is greater than that of their peers.

The normal five senses can be separated into two categories: direct and indirect. The indirect senses are hearing and sight which measure intensities of wave energy. The direct senses are taste, touch, and smell which measure the physical qualities of objects through direct contact. Usually the five senses produce compatible data, but sometimes they fail to do so, as when the artist's illusion of perspective fools the eye but not the touch.

Each sense operates on a separate plane, perceiving a distinct quality of existence. These planes are extremely limited. Human sight and hearing, for example, measure only a tiny range of wave energy. The eyes cannot see invisible frequencies of light and many sounds are pitched too high or too low for the human ear to hear. The same is true of the indirect senses. We'll never know what it is like to smell infinitesimal scents as a bloodhound does, or how to taste a river bed with our entire bodies, like a catfish. In fact, we exist in an environment that is far richer than our normal senses are able to perceive.

Let's suppose, for the sake of argument, that other parts of our body can sense elements in this rich environment that we otherwise would not be able to perceive. This is in fact the case with subsonic frequencies, which affect our nervous systems directly, causing us to become nervous and edgy. Movie producers use this "sixth sense" to enhance the experience of terror in adventure and horror movies. Perhaps this is not be the only way our bodies can sense energy otherwise imperceptible to our normal senses. If visions of Angels are reactions to some exterior stimulus, then the receptor of this sixth sense may be the brain itself.

The brain is an extremely sensitive organ connected directly to the nervous system, which is the conduit of the other five senses. We are used to thinking of the brain as an active organ—we use it to think and create. Isn't it possible that the brain might also be a passive organ capable of sensing energy, just like the eyes and ears? If this is the case, visions of Angels might very well be the result of the mind being directly stimulated by energies that lie outside the realm of the five senses.

While this is pure speculation, it provides a good explanation as to why Angels might appear in such different ways to people in different cultures. If it is indeed a passive sense organ, the brain may combine this receptive function with its more active behaviors. It is likely that whatever the brain perceives will get mingled with other thoughts and ideas in the consciousness, so that a person who sees Angels adapts the "vision" to fit his or her own cultural biases and personal preconceptions.

ABRAHAM AND THE THREE ANGELS

It is not automatically absurd that a source of Angelic energy might appear to a Christian as the Archangel Michael, to a Taoist as a mountain god, or to a jungle shaman as the lord of the forest. What is actually being seen is a source of energy that the human mind has clothed in the light of its own familiar perception and memory.

So are Angels real? The answer is that they are probably as real as anything else. If Angels exist, they do so on a plane of energy that is perceived directly by the brain, with its natural tendency to interpret that energy in highly individual and culturally specific ways. The question now becomes: why and how should this energy appear as an Angel and not as a point of light, or a feeling, or a particular scent?

In fact, all of these interpretations have been reported as phenomena connected with Angelic contact. If the brain is being stimulated, the response to the stimulus apparently takes different forms. This, in itself, does not argue against the reality of the experience, merely that the phenomenon is a complex one and that the brain has various ways to interpret the energy it perceives.

❧

How Do Angels Appear?

As we've already discussed, Angels often appear to people in their dreams. During sleep, the brain is in a receptive state. In that state, the Angelic energy manifests itself as a dream vision that instructs the dreamer in how to handle a particular situation.

This is one case where I can speak from personal experience. From time to time, the figure of a wise old woman has appeared in my dreams and helped me deal with difficult emotional situations. Sometimes this woman appears as my grandmother and other times as an amazingly aged, but wonderfully kind black woman. Each time this figure has appeared to me, it has given me a key to making an important change in my life. In one case, I was told how to get closer to my family. In another case, I was told that I needed to disconnect from a relationship that had become extremely limiting. I have no idea whether these experiences are merely dreams or are actually perceptions of something exterior to my mind. From my own selfish perspective, it really doesn't matter very much. The fact that the experiences have been subjectively real and, most importantly, useful, outweighs the question of whether the experiences are actually "real." The point is that I learned something and took action as a result.

Angels also appear as visions to the waking mind. Unlike dreams, these experiences sometimes are shared by more than one person. The most famous example of this is the Angel of Mons.[4] Thousands of Allied soldiers saw Angels in the sky during this critical battle of World War I. The Mons event is well documented and bears certain similarities to UFO sightings, where large groups of people, in different locations, see *something* in the sky.

Perhaps the most interesting way that Angels are said to appear is in the form of a living, breathing human being who has powers that are beyond normal human abilities. This type of phenomenon is surprisingly common, and the people who have claimed to have had such experiences are often quite reliable in other ways. Many of them are not even religious.

Are these people really seeing Angels? These contact experiences seem to be quite different from the dreams and visions that characterize other types of Angel sightings; and seem to imply that Angels are just like you and me—composed of physical material rather than some form of energy.

Are Angels really spirits at all? This is not a new question. For many years theologians battled over the essential nature of the Angels, some arguing that Angels were entirely spiritual, others arguing that Angels were composed of material substance. The notion that Angels are forms of energy is not incompatible with the notion that they sometimes appear in human form. If Angels are directly perceived by the human brain, then a dream or a vision is a case of that energy influencing the mind. If an energy source (Angel) can cause the brain to see images, then it might also be able to influence the brain to a much higher degree: The Angel might be able to take control of the body and cause behavior quite different from normal.

This is, in fact, a very common religious belief. In many cultures, Shamans and priests are believed to be able to call gods and Angels into themselves, at which point they become a living manifestation of that aspect of the divine energy. The same thing is believed to happen in cases of demonic possession, only the invasion is involuntary and the energy is an undesirable one. A more modern example of this belief is "channeling," where a medium takes on the personality of a spiritual being and provides advice to friends and family.

According to many accounts, cases of possession often are accompanied by unusual physical phenomena. Reports of objects flying across the room, glass breaking at a distance and other poltergeist events are common. In seances, participants sometimes claim to experience telekinetic activity, such as the rising of tables. While it is true that these phenomena can be faked by a clever charlatan, it does not follow that every instance is automatically a fake.

I have seen some amazing things in my life, many of which are difficult or impossible to explain according to the precepts of western science. For example, I recently walked barefoot across a forty-foot bed of two-thousand-degree embers without damaging my feet. This is, I am told, a scientific impossibility, and yet I certainly experienced it. While I do not believe that I was possessed by an Angel when I did it, I was certainly in a very unusual mental and emotional state.

The Greeks and the Romans believed that certain highly favored human beings were touched by divine energy. They were said to be "possessed of their genius"—their highest divine self. Seen this way, there is no inconsistency between the idea of an Angel appearing as a dream or vision and an Angel appearing as a physical being. It is simply a matter of degree. In the first two cases, the Angelic influence is relatively minor, although the experience may be a quite moving one. In the case of physical manifestations, the Angelic energy possesses a human being who then manifests the Angelic energy.

WHAT IS ANGEL MAGIC?

In dreams, visions, and Angelic possessions, the role of the human is basically a passive one. The Angels come and go as they please, dispensing wisdom and assistance seemingly at their own pleasure. Angel Magic, on the other hand, is an ancient art that allows humans to initiate contact with Angels (whenever it seems necessary or prudent) through rituals, prayers and practices that summon Angels to earth.

While belief in Angel Magic is compatible with religious beliefs, the purpose of Angel Magic is quite different from the purpose of religious prayer. Sir James George Frazer, in the landmark anthropology text, *The Golden Bough*, makes this distinction quite clear. The nature of religion is worship. It is passive. The prayers that are offered to God are humble requests. Angel Magic is something altogether different. Angel Magic implies control.[5]

Angel Magic as we know it today is based largely on a number of manuscripts that were copied and recopied in the medieval and Renaissance periods. These manuscripts, known as "grimoires," contained complex rituals believed to have the power to summon Angels. Because Angel Magic ran contrary to the teaching of the church, only a few of these Angel Magic grimoires were published prior to this century. Figure 1 shows the title page of the first known grimoire ever published, a book of Angel Magic dated 1565. No publisher was named, because publishing Angel Magic rituals was dangerous to all concerned. (See the Suggested Reading at the back of this book for a list of grimoires published within the past thirty years.)

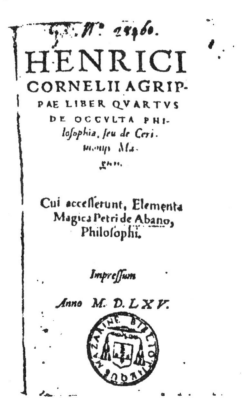

FIGURE I. TITLE PAGE OF RENAISSANCE GRIMOIRE[6]

An "Angel Magus" is a person who practices Angel Magic. An Angel Magus is very different from a priest who is, by necessity, tied to the theological notion that some Angels are good and others are evil. The Angel Magus tends to categorize Angels as useful and not useful. This is why so many of the grimoires—even those that have been highly Christianized—include methods for summoning devils as well as Angels. The Angel Magus is more interested in controlling Angels and obtaining a particular outcome than in the ethical stance of the Angel involved.

According to the grimoires, different Angels have different characteristics, powers, and abilities. Grimoires usually contain exhaustive lists of Angelic names, each corresponding to one of the planets, the constellations, the four elements, various parts of the world, and even the hours of the day. By using these lists, the Angel Magus can choose, with great precision, the type and quality of the Angel to be contacted.

Above this mass of lesser Angels are the mighty Angels of legend. In the western tradition, the more powerful Angels are Michael, Uriel and Gabriel. The names of these Angels are very old, harkening back to early Hebraic religion. The term "El"—in which all three names terminate—was an ancient Hebrew name for God and the Elohim were believed to be his chief servants. According to tradition, it takes a very powerful magician to control such entities. Even Doctor John Dee—arguably the greatest Angel Magus of all time—tended to be uneasy in their presence.

The two basic principles of Angel Magic come from two sources: the folk beliefs of many cultures and the Hebrew Cabala.

The first principle of Angel Magic is the belief that humans can control Angels through the use of magical weapons. This belief is found nearly everywhere in the world. For example:

- At the southern tip of South America, the Patagonians used to try to dispel the demon of smallpox by "slashing the air with their weapons and throwing water about in order to keep off the dreadful pursuer."

- At the northern tip of North America, the Eskimos have their "young women and girls drive the spirit out of every house with their knives, stabbing viciously under the bunks and deer-skins and calling upon [the demons] to be gone."

- Among the heathen Wotyaks, a Finnish people of Eastern Russia, "all the young girls of the village assemble on the last day of the year, armed with sticks, the ends of which are split in nine places. With these they beat every corner of the house and yard, saying 'We are driving Satan out of the village.'"

- In Australia, the aborigines drive away devils by beating the ground with the stuffed tail of a kangaroo.[7]

The second principle of Angel Magic is the belief that certain words—especially the names of God—have the power to constrain Angels to obey the will of the Angel Magus. This principle is based upon the Hebrew Cabala which says that the name of an object is inextricably linked with that object. To know the true name of something is to be able to control it completely. This belief was so strong that the Jews refused to speak or write the name of God—"YHVH."

Instead, they masked this holy name behind a complicated set of symbols and substitutions. The real name of God was supposed to consist of seventy-two letters, and be so powerful that the world would be destroyed if anybody actually pronounced it.

According to the Angel Magi, a human correctly armed with a sacred weapon and sacred words can control the most powerful Angels in heaven, in hell, or on the earth. There is, however, more to Angel Magic than this. Angel Magic is a set of formal rituals that contains five basic steps:

1. *Consecration.* The Magus builds a temple in which to practice the magical ceremony. In most cases, this consists of a magical circle, marked with holy names and/or objects, as shown in Figure 2.

2. *Invocation.* The Magus offers a prayer to the highest level of the Godhead, in effect raising his or her consciousness.

3. *Conjuration.* The Magus uses a combination of divine names, magical weaponry and offerings of incense to cause the Angel to appear.

4. *Conversation.* Once the Angel has appeared, the Magus describes and records what the Angel does and says.

5. *Dismissal.* The Angel Magus dismisses the Angel from the area or sets it to perform a certain task.

These five elements are found in nearly all of the grimoires. The ceremonies are often complex, containing exhaustive instructions, requirements, and preconditions, all of which are said to be essential to successful completion of the work.

FIGURE 2. MAGICAL CIRCLE FROM A RENAISSANCE GRIMOIRE[8]

In addition to the five basic steps of Angel Magic, there are five
major elements that appear in almost all the grimoires. These are the
lowest common denominator of Angel Magic ceremonies, and we will
look at each of them in detail.

1. *Incantations.* These are specialized prayers that use the
   power of the Angelic names to summon the Angels
   themselves. The purpose of the incantation is to associate
   the minds of the participants with the divine energy of
   the Angel being summoned. The Angel Magus chants a
   series of divine names that compel the Angel to appear.
   This is part of the Cabala, which maintains that words
   and the things they represent are one and the same.
   Under this logic, a holy name or a name of god or Angel

borrows the power of that god or Angel. This concept is not limited to the Cabala. It is reflected in the New Testament, which begins with the statement, "In the beginning was the word." It is also reflected in the Koran:

> *And Allah taught Adam all the names, then showed them to the Angels, saying: "Inform Me of the names of these, if ye are truthful." The Angels said: "Be glorified! We have no knowledge except that which Thou hast taught us." And when Adam had informed the Angels of their names, he said: "Did I not tell you that I know the secret of the heavens and the earth? And I know that which ye disclose and which ye hide."*[9]

2. *Weapons.* Magical weapons compel Angels to obey the Magus who wields them. This is intended to be useful for fallen Angels who might otherwise prove unruly. The well-armed Angel Magus has two primary weapons — the staff and the sword, or knife.

FIGURE 3. ANGEL MAGIC KNIFE FROM A RENAISSANCE GRIMOIRE[10]

3. *Scrying.* A scryer is a person who can see and hear Angels
in a crystal stone, black mirror, in the fires of a flame, or
in the swirling smoke of heavy incense. The term "scryer"
has the same root as the nearly obsolete verb "to descry,"
which means "to see clearly." A scryer is not the same as a
medium. A medium in a channeling trance believes that
he or she is actually possessed by the entity, which then
speaks through the medium's mouth. The scryer remains
aloof from the experience, seeing and hearing Angels as if
they were on display. This is not to say Angel Magi don't
use mediums. According to some sources it is actually
easier to get Angels to manifest inside a human medium
than it is to make the Angels appear inside a crystal.

However, there appear to be certain dangers inherent in
mediumship, almost as if the human mind were insuffi-
cient to contain the powers of the Angels that the Magus
summons. This is especially true if the Angel Magus is
working alone and must act as his or her own scryer. It
would be a disaster, from the viewpoint of the Magus, if
the Angel actually entered and controlled the Magus'
body. That would break the pattern of the ceremony and
likely make it impossible for the Magus to record whatever the Angel wanted to communicate.

4. *Talismans.* A talisman is a physical object that an Angel
has energized with its unique form of divine energy. Just
as the holy names have the power to summon Angels,
talismans engraved with divine names and correctly
energized have magical power.

There are two types of talismans in Angel Magic: protective and practical. Protective talismans are believed to

keep the Angel Magus safe when conjuring Angels whose power is difficult to control or particularly dangerous to human beings. Practical talismans are created by the Angel Magus to store a portion of the psychic energy of the Angel so that it can be used at a later date. For example, an Angel Magus might engrave a pen with sigils sacred to the planet Mercury, and then invoke a mercurial Angel into the pen so that the Magus will be inspired to write beautiful prose.

The application of talismans is limited only by the imagination of the Angel Magus; and the grimoires spend a great deal of time explaining how to make and use them. (A set of planetary talismans, never before published in book form in the United States, is given in the Appendix of this book.)

5. *Incense.* Believed to give the Angel something out of which to construct a temporary material form, incense recipes are included in many of the grimoires. In ancient times the use of incense was often supplemented by some kind of animal sacrifice. It was believed that the energy of the dying animal would provide energy to the Angel so that it could more easily manifest.

Angel Magic is a set of rituals by which a human can obtain a vision of an Angelic being. Over the years, Angel Magic has acquired a complex array of ideas and symbols drawn from astrology, alchemy, theology and even modern psychology. The growth and transformation of Angel Magic over the centuries is one of the most interesting developments in the history of human thought. Here, for the first time, is the complete story.

CONFERENCE WITH THE ANGEL RAPHAEL

The Source
of Angel Magic

here has always been a great deal of controversy surrounding the origins of Angel Magic. Because it existed outside of the accepted teaching of the Christian Church, there are not as many historical references as we would like. Dating individual manuscripts and Angel Magic rituals is as much a matter of intuition as it is of evidence.

The Angel Magi of the Renaissance believed that Angel Magic was among the oldest forms of worship known to mankind. To quote the reputed Renaissance Angel Magus Paracelsus, "Conjurations…had their original Spring and fountain from Babylon; and there did mightily increase and flourish, afterwards it came into Aegypt, and from thence to the Israelites, and last of all, to us Christians."[1]

When scholars and occultists started publishing the grimoires at the end of the nineteenth century, some of them accepted the traditional dating. When Macgregor Mathers published his translation of the *Key of Solomon*, he attributed the work to Solomon himself.[2] While this may not have been intended to be taken seriously, Mathers clearly believed that the rituals in their original form must be very old indeed. Another student of Angel Magic, A.E. Waite, responded in his *Book of Ceremonial Magic* that the medieval rituals were obviously modern in presentation.[3] He thought it highly unlikely that the rituals inside the grimoires could be as old as Mathers believed them to be.

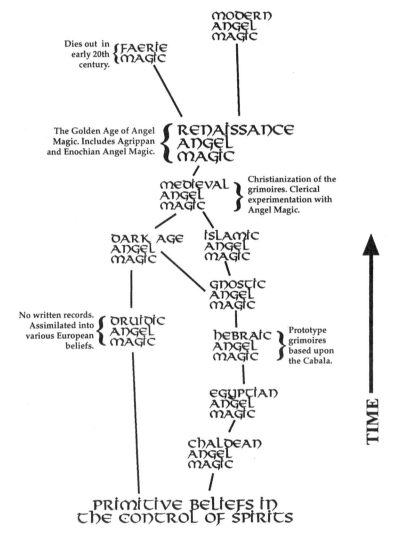

FIGURE 4. THE HERITAGE OF ANGEL MAGIC

The truth lies in between. Certain elements of the Angel Magic rituals are clearly quite old and some elements might even date from Egyptian Angel Magic over three thousand years ago. On the other hand, the form and structure of the grimoires are clearly medieval. The rituals were collected and edited and amended by medieval clerics, and they reflect the scholarly thinking of the men of that time. The true heritage of Angel Magic is shown in Figure 4.

CHALDEAN ANGEL MAGIC

The earliest recorded Angel Magic rituals in existence today were composed in ancient Chaldea around 3000 B.C., and later recorded on stone tablets. As old as these incantations are, they contain many elements that are found in the medieval grimoires:

> *The seven gods of the vast heavens,*
> *The seven gods of the great earth,*
> *The seven gods of the igneous spheres,*
> *The seven gods, these are the seven gods,*
> 5 *The seven malevolent gods,*
> *The seven malevolent phantoms,*
> *The seven malevolent phantoms of the flames,*
> *in the heavens, seven, on the earth, seven.*
> *The wicked demon, the wicked Atal,*
> *the wicked Gigim,*
> *The wicked Tetal, the wicked god,*
> *the wicked Maskim*

10   Spirit of the heavens, conjure!

      Spirit of the earth, conjure!

      Spirit of Mul-ge, king of the countries, conjure!

      Spirit of Nin-gelal, lady of the countries, conjure!

      Spirit of Nin-dar, son of the zenith, conjure!

15   Spirit of Tiskhu, lady of the countries,

            which shines in the night, conjure![4]

Lines one through three describe the gods (Angels) of the planets, who live in the "vast heavens," rule the "great earth" (the universe), and are gods of the "igneous spheres" (the celestial spheres of the planets themselves). That there are only seven gods (and not twenty-one) is shown by the summary in line four, "these are the seven gods." Lines five through seven describe the seven evil gods, who in Chaldean mythology rebelled against the seven planetary gods and fell to earth. Thus in total there are "in the heavens, seven," and "on the earth, seven." Lines eight and nine give the names of the four most powerful of the seven evil gods, Alal, Gigim, Tetal, and Maskim. Lines ten through fifteen give the divine names of the planetary Angels Mulge, Nin-gelal, Nin-dar, and Tiskhu, which represent the Sun, the Moon, Jupiter, and Venus, respectively.

Despite the age of this incantation, it possesses many of the characteristics of the conjurations in ritual systems of a much later date. First, the Angels are associated with the planets, just as in the medieval grimoires. Second, we see the appearance of the belief that divine names of higher Angels give control over lesser Angels.

FIGURE 5. CHALDEAN ANGEL (FROM ARCHEOLOGICAL RUINS)[5]

EGYPTIAN ANGEL MAGIC

Other cultures borrowed Chaldean concepts, uniting them to their own mythologies and theologies. The Egyptians also believed that Angels (gods) could be controlled by invoking the power of the names of greater Angels. They also believed that an Angel Magus could be exalted into near-divine status through certain rituals and prayers. The Egyptians elevated priests and pharaohs above the native spirits, giving man a place in the hierarchy of the Angels.[6] Because a human could be an Angel, it was believed that he could control lesser Angels, much as a king could command lesser men.

It was the Egyptians who began the use of mysterious magical names as part of their Angel Magic prayers. This can be seen in the following excerpt from an Egyptian papyrus:

Take a clean linen bag and write upon it the names given below. Fold it up and make it into a lamp-wick and set it alight, pouring pure oil over it. The word to be written is this: "Armiuth. Lailamchouch, Arsenophrephren. Phtha, Archentechtha." [7]

Egyptian Angel Magic was connected to astrology, and featured paraphernalia such as wands, incense, and sacrifices. The Egyptians believed that Angels could appear in any number of different ways:

- in a statue or in an image
- in a talisman
- in a dream
- in a trance (sometimes induced by drugs)
- as a phantom or as a disincarnate voice
- in a human or animal body (possession)
- in a human or animal corpse (necromancy)
- as an invisible or selectively invisible being.

FIGURE 6. EGYPTIAN ANGEL MAGUS[8]

Figure 6 shows what appears to be an Egyptian Angel Magus invoking an Angel into a statue. The Magus is wearing some sort of animal skin and holds a curved wand or club.

Several examples of Egyptian Angel Magic have survived until modern times. One Egyptian papyrus gives a ritual of Angel Magic probably dating from earlier than 1000 B.C.:

> *To obtain a vision from Bes. Make a drawing of Besa, as shown below, on your left hand, and envelope your hand in a strip of black cloth around your neck. The ink with which you write must be composed of the blood of a cow, the blood of a white dove, fresh frankincense, myrrh, black writing-ink, cinnabar, mulberry juice, rain-water and the juice of wormwood and vetch. With this write your petition before the setting sun, [saying] "send the truthful seer out of the holy shrine, I beseech thee Lampsuer, Sumarta, Baribas, Dardalam, Iorlex: O Lord send the sacred deity Anuth, Anuth, Salbana, Chambre, Breith, now now, quickly, quickly. Come in this very night."* [9]

Once again we see elements of Angel Magic that appear in the medieval grimoires. The drawing of an image on the hand is immediately suggestive of Angelic talismans contained in the grimoires, and the god Besa, a bestial dwarf, is similar in form to the medieval descriptions of fallen Angels. Incense, herbs, and ink made from animal blood are also mentioned in the medieval grimoires. Egyptian Angel Magic had to be worked at a specific time of the day; similar restrictions are described in the grimoires. Furthermore, the magical names in the Egyptian ritual closely resemble the cabalistic names included in the grimoires.

So here we have clear evidence that Angel Magic, in the form it was practiced in the Renaissance, had its roots deep in the religious practices of ancient Egypt.

MEDIEVAL ANGEL

◦◦◦

Hebraic Angel Magic

The ancient Hebrews picked up where the Egyptians left off, formalizing and improving the practice of Angel Magic, mixing in elements of the Cabala and Jewish mysticism. Much of the Hebraic legends about Angel Magic is tied to various stories about King Solomon, who was reputed to have commanded Angels to do his mighty will. In *The Book of Wisdom*, a Gnostic text attributed to Solomon, we find the following description of Solomon's Angel Magic:

> *Wielding the weapons of his sacred office, prayer and aton-*
> *ing incense…not by physical strength, not by force of arms;*
> *but by word he prevailed over the Punisher [avenging*
> *Angel] by recalling the weapons of his sacred office, prayer*
> *and atoning incense…not by physical strength, not by force*
> *of arms; but by word he prevailed over the Punisher [aveng-*
> *ing Angel] by recalling the oaths made to the Fathers…the*
> *whole world was on his flowing robe, the glorious names of*
> *the Fathers on the four rows of stones, and your Majesty*
> *(YHVH) on the diadem on his head."*[10]

This passage suggests a well-defined system of ritual Angel Magic which included sacred weapons, prayers, oaths and incantations, a robe embroidered with arcane symbols meant to represent the universe, and a crown with YHVH written upon it. All of these elements are present in the medieval grimoires. The grimoire known as the *Key of Solomon*, for example, includes magical weaponry,[11] and its incantations and conjurations tell of the oaths made to the Hebrew fathers.[12] The garments in the Key include a robe embroidered with arcane symbols, and a paper crown with YHVH written on the front.[13]

Hebraic Angel Magic talismans were constructed of metal and often combined with herbs or leaves. In this passage from Josephus, a Jewish historian of the first century A.D., we find a curious combination of folk herbology and Angel Magic:

> *He did put unto the nose of the possessed a ring, under the scale whereof was enclosed a kind of roote, whose virtue Solomon declared, and the savor thereof drew the devil out at his nose; so as down fell the man...Eleazar (the mage) made mention of Solomon, reciting conjurations of Solomon's own making.*[14]

Solomon was not the only Hebrew sage believed to have practiced Angel Magic. A fourth century A.D. manuscript known as the *Sword of Moses* contains a brief description of an Angel Magic ritual attributed to Moses:

> *To conjure a spirit, write on a laurel-leaf "I conjure the prince, whose name is Abraksas, in the name of* לאשבוצי *that thou comest to me and revealest all that I ask of thee and thou shalt not tarry.*[15]

The ancient Hebrews maintained that if a man knew the secret name of YHVH, he would be able to work miracles otherwise reserved for YHVH Himself. A section of the conjurations in the *Sword of Moses* illustrates the similarity of Hebraic Magic to the incantations of the Chaldeans:

> *My wish be fulfilled, and my word hearkened unto, and my prayer received through the conjuration with the Ineffable name of God, which is glorified in the world, through which all the heavenly hosts are tied and bound. I conjure you that you shall not refuse me nor hurt me, nor frighten and alarm me, in the tremendous name of your King, the terror of whom rests upon you.*[16]

The Hebrews probably inherited the belief in Angel Magic from their Egyptian overlords. The magical powers attributed to Moses and Aaron in the Bible suggest that the interest of the Jews in Magic probably began during the period of captivity. The necromancy of the witch of Endor,[17] too, indicates a belief in the power of people to conjure supernatural beings.

The development of Hebraic Angel Magic is linked to the development of the Cabala. The Hebrews transformed the magical incantations of the Egyptian rituals into a complex numerology and into a belief that God was manifested as a word. By knowing the secret names of God, a Magus could control the spirits and Angels that served Him.[18]

There are many similarities between the medieval grimoires and the much older text of the *Sword of Moses*. The comparison is a particularly interesting one because the Sword of Moses, unlike the grimoires, was not transmitted into Europe during the dark ages, but instead survived in Syria in its original form. Both the *Key* and the *Sword* are attributed to the Jewish sages who were revered as magicians. Both open their texts with a description of the death of the author, and with the process by which the magical system was preserved. The preparatory rituals of the *Key* and the *Sword* are almost identical. From the *Sword*:

> *The man who decides to use it must first free himself three days previously from accidental pollution and from everything unclean, eat and drink once every evening, and must eat the bread from a pure man, or wash his hands first in salt [?] and drink only water...pray three times daily, and after each prayer recite the following blessing: 'Blessed art thou, O Lord our God, King of the Universe....'[19]*

From the *Key*:

> *During the last three days before the commencement of*
> *this action thou shalt content thyself with only eating*
> *fasting diet, and that only once in the day; and it will*
> *be better still if thou only partakest of bread and water.*
> *Thou shalt also abstain from every impure thing, recit-*
> *ing the prayer above written.*

The prayer in question, like the one in the *Sword*, begins, "O Lord
God, the Father Eternal...."[20]

The *Sword* mentions a seal written on a laurel leaf which is used for
conjuring a spirit,[21] an element similar to the seals in the *Key*. Both
books use herbs and charms to procure magical effects. Both deal with
the conjuring of Angels and devils. This is logical because, according to
Hebrew mythology, both good and evil Angels are subservient to God.[22]
Through the power of the magician's incantations, which contain the
sacred names of God, the magician can control good and evil spirits, or
perform either benign or malevolent deeds through his Magic.

Other grimoires, such as the *Sepher Raziel* and the *Lemegeton*, also
contain elements of great antiquity; however, their texts have been
confused with later additions. Portions of the *Sepher Raziel* may be as
old as the *Key of Solomon*.[23] The *Lemegeton*, however, has undergone
vast Christianization. Despite this, certain of the seals of the *Goetia*,
which is the first section of the *Lemegeton*, resemble the inscriptions
on ancient monuments,[24] suggesting that the antiquity of the *Lemege-*
ton is far greater than has generally been assumed.

S	A	T	O	R
A	R	E	P	O
T	E	N	E	T
O	P	E	R	A
R	O	T	A	S

FIGURE 7. THE SATOR/ROTAS MAGICAL SQUARE[25]

Another ancient item of Angel Magic is the *Sator-Rotas* magical square shown in Figure 7. The earliest example of this acrostic can be found on a wall in Herculaneum, one of the cities destroyed by Mt. Vesuvius in A.D. 79. Underneath the square was an inscription sacred to the god Saturn. The *Key of Solomon* contains a talisman sacred to the planet Saturn which is built around the *Sator-Rotas* square.

This magical square might originally have been Hebrew. One of the later grimoires, *The Sacred Magic of Abramelin the Mage*, gives a variation based upon Hebrew words, as shown in Figure 8.

S	A	L	O	M
A	R	E	P	O
L	E	M	E	L
O	P	E	R	A
M	O	L	A	S

FIGURE 8. MODIFIED SATOR/ROTAS MAGICAL SQUARE[26]

These similarities suggest that the medieval grimoires share their origins with texts like the *Sword of Moses*. Despite the errors of translators and copyists and the editorial additions from a later date, we have a case where the essential elements of some very old magical ceremonies have survived into comparatively modern times.

❧

GNOSTIC ANGEL MAGIC

The rituals of Angel Magic spread from the middle east into other regions of the world. The Eleusian and similar mystery cults probably practiced the art in their inner orders. The Zoroastrian Magi and the Pythagoreans were widely revered as magicians, and the priests of Serapis and Mithras may also have been involved in Angel Magic rituals.[27] Despite the atmosphere of secrecy that surrounded these cults, the basic premise of Angel Magic—that man could control spirits through the power of prayer—was universally accepted in pre-Christian times. The universal acceptance of these beliefs can be gauged by the practice of exorcism to treat mental illness, a practice that was common throughout the Mediterranean.

The Gnostic sects of the Christians were particularly attracted to the practice of Angel Magic. The Gnostics were a sect of early Christians who tried to unite Christian doctrine to the older traditions of Paganism. The Gnostics were also influenced by the Zoroastrians and the Essenes. Gnosticism tended to develop in the eastern parts of the Roman Empire. Because the Gnostics were closer geographically and theologically to the traditions of the East, they more easily accepted the practice of Angel Magic than the more skeptical branches of the church in the West.

The Gnostics built their belief in Angel Magic upon biblical references to Jesus' ability to control devils. Jesus even states (Mark 16:7) that his name, like that of YHVH, has the power to control demons. That some form of Angel Magic was practiced in the early Christian church is quite likely; however, the attitude of the early church towards Angel Magic eventually became hostile and it disappeared, at least for a while, from standard Christian dogma.

A passage from the Acts of the Apostles illustrates the ambivalence of the early church towards Angel Magic:

> Some itinerant Jewish exorcists tried pronouncing the name of the Lord Jesus over people who were possessed by evil spirits; they used to say, "I command you by the Jesus whose spokesman is Paul..." The evil spirit replied, "Jesus I recognize, and I know who Paul is, but who are you?" And the man with the evil spirit hurled himself at them and overpowered first one, and then another, and handled them so violently that they ran from that house naked and badly mauled.[28]

The story of the gifts of the Magi also suggests that Jesus' biographers realized the debt that he owed to the Zoroastrian Magi, who inherited and preserved the ancient Chaldean rituals. It is interesting, in this respect, to note that both the Chaldean incantations and Jesus' exorcisms were primarily medicinal in purpose.

Gnostic Angel Magic continues with the Hebraic themes, providing many of the elements found in the medieval grimoires. An ancient Gnostic text, referred to as the "Untitled Apocalypse," contains the following promise to Gnostic devotees:

> Be steadfast in My word, and I will give you eternal life and send you powers, and I will strengthen you in spirits of power, and give you authority according to your will. And no one shall hinder you in what ye desire and ye shall beget for yourselves aeons, worlds, and heavens, in order that the

> *mind-born spirits may come and dwell therein. And ye will*
> *be gods, and will know that ye come from God...*[29]

In this passage, knowledge of the ineffable name ("My word") grants the control of "mind-born spirits" (Angels created in the mind of God). The aeons, worlds and heavens which the magician is to "beget" are most likely representations of the universe seals and talismans in which the spirits are to dwell. The relationship of Gnostic Angel Magic to previous systems can be discerned in the assumption that by assimilating himself into the Godhead through the use of the ineffable name, the Angel Magus can gain divine status.

By contrast, the orthodox branches of the church looked upon the practice of Angel Magic with a certain amount of distaste. Their own cultures possessed only the most primitive form of spirit control.[30] The mystical aspirations of the Gnostic magician seemed foreign and bizarre, and the "mind-born spirits" were too much like the old gods of the Pagans.

FIGURE 9. ANGELS FROM LATE GNOSTIC MANUSCRIPT[31]

The tale about the meeting of St. Paul and Simon Magus, the supposed founder of Gnosticism, illustrates this skeptical attitude. Simon Magus was reputed to have a panoply of magical skills[32] including:

- Making himself invisible

- Creating a man out of air

- Passing through rocks and mountains without encountering an obstacle

- Throwing himself from a precipice uninjured

- Flying in the air

- Flinging himself in fire without being burned

- Breaking through bolts and chains

- Animating statues, so that they appeared to every beholder to be men and women

- Making the furniture in the house to change places

- Changing his countenance and visage into that of another

- Making himself into a sheep, a goat, or a serpent

- Walking through the streets attended with a multitude of strange figures, which he affirmed to be the souls of the departed

- Making trees and branches suddenly to spring up wherever he pleased

- Setting up and deposing kings at will

- Causing a sickle to go into a field of corn, which unassisted would mow twice as fast as the most industrious reaper

When asked to demonstrate his power to St. Paul, Simon commanded his spirit servants to lift him above the earth. St. Paul, however, ordered the spirits to drop the Magus, which they did, causing his death.[33] This magical duel is perhaps symbolic of the conflict between the established church and the Gnostic heresy.

Although the basic premises of Angel Magic were among the teachings of Christ, and the ancient rituals had been adapted by the Gnostics to Christian mythology, the established church eventually rejected the belief that man could become like an Angel and command other Angels.

This did not keep the Gnostics from developing Angel Magic into a complex system of rituals and prayer. They introduced magical squares into the tradition of Angel Magic. Figure 10 shows a Gnostic magical square that was believed to give the bearer power not only over Angels, but over other humans as well.

α	ε	η	ι	ο	υ	ω
ε	η	ι	ο	υ	ω	α
η	ι	ο	υ	ω	α	ε
ι	ο	υ	ω	α	ε	η
ο	υ	ω	α	ε	η	ι
υ	ω	α	ε	η	ι	ο
ω	α	ε	η	ι	ο	υ

FIGURE 10. GNOSTIC MAGICAL SQUARE[34]

FIGURE 11. GNOSTIC MAGICAL TALISMAN[35]

The Gnostics also seem to have been the first magicians to use secret alphabets to preserve the sanctity of the magical names. Previous to the time of the Gnostics, such secrecy was probably unnecessary due to the general illiteracy of the public. One of the earliest examples of a magical alphabet appears on a Gnostic artifact of the third century A.D. The talisman engraved on it (Figure 11) forms a substantial link between Gnostic talismans and the medieval grimoires. The three outer circles are separated into thirty-two segments, each representing a different letter of the Greek alphabet. The characters inside each segment are esoteric forms of the letter, intended for use only among initiates. Several shapes are given for many of the letters, possibly indicating a sophisticated rotational code, where the first occurrence of a letter is replaced by the first form, the second occurrence by the second form, etc., until all available choices have been used.

The inner circle contains an incantation that immediately suggests a kinship with the Greek acrostic given in Figure 10. The words, when written out, appear to be a howling or keening sound. The characters in the inner circle are directly related to characters and talismans found in the grimoires. The glyph of a man with outstretched arms is identical to glyphs that are linked to the central figure in the Secret Seal of Solomon (Figure 12) given in the *Lemegeton*. Note that this seal is also surrounded by alphabetic characters. Other glyphs in the central circle of the artifact bear a curious resemblance to the characters in the famous Pentacle of Solomon also from the *Lemegeton* (Figure 13).

FIGURE 12. SECRET SEAL OF SOLOMON[36]

FIGURE 13. PENTACLE OF SOLOMON[37]

Gnostic jewelry often contained the divine names of Hebraic Magic. The Gnostics also developed talismans that used geometric configurations to express power over Angels. This was part of an over-all movement away from the simple talismans of the Hebrews, Egyptians and Chaldeans to the complex graphic representations found in later works on Angel Magic.

Eventually the established church decided that the Gnostic heresy constituted a threat. The magicians of the late Gnostic period were subject to great persecutions. The military machinery of the Christianized Roman Empire was mobilized to destroy temples, murder Gnostic priests, and burn heretical documents.* By the sixth century, Gnosticism had been nearly eradicated, and with it much of the Gnostic tradition of Angel Magic. This fall from grace, however, was to prove only temporary.

---

* It is perhaps ironic that the same military strength that permitted and promoted the crucifix-ion should be used by the established church to persecute a Christian sect whose doctrines may have more closely resembled Christ's original teachings.

FROM THE REVELATION OF ST. JOHN

The Survival
of Angel Magic

ngel Magic fell into disrepute in Western Europe. It ceased to be part of the religious teachings of the established church and those who practiced it were persecuted as heretics. This is not to say that people completely disbelieved the idea that humans could control Angels; it was just that these teachings were now considered Pagan rather than Christian, and the Angels thus conjured and controlled were assumed to be devils.

DARK AGE ANGEL MAGIC

This idea can be seen clearly in a popular tale about Merlin that dates from the dark ages. According to this story, Merlin conceived a project for surrounding his native town of Caermarthen with a wall of brass. He committed to the execution of this project a multitude of spirits, who labored underground in a neighboring cavern. It was about this time that Merlin was entrapped in his tomb by the Lady of the Lake. Meanwhile the fiends, at work in the cavern, and remembering their master's commands not to suspend their labors until his return, continued in their labors forever. The traveler who passes that way, if he lays his ear close to the mouth of the cavern, will hear a ghastly noise of iron chains and brazen caldrons, the loud strokes of the hammer, and the ringing sound of the anvil, intermixed with the pants and groans of the workmen. It is said that this is enough to unsettle the brain of any who is so brave or foolish as to listen to the din.

Another reputed Angel Magus of the Dark Ages was Saint Dunstan, an early church figure associated with the Abbey at Glastonbury where King Arthur was reputed to have been buried. Dunstan, so the story goes, spent his early years hanging around prostitutes and living a sinful life. Despite this, he was said to be a person of extraordinary intelligence and high ambition, who swiftly acquired any talent or art upon which he fixed his attention. At one point he contracted a dangerous illness that baffled his physicians. While he lay at the point of death, an Angel was seen bringing him medicine that cured him instantly. The future saint immediately rose from his bed and hastened to the nearest church to thank God for his recovery. On his way, he had a vision of the devil, surrounded by a pack of black dogs, which tried to keep him from the church. Dunstan brandished a rod that he held in his hand driving the vision away.[1]

What is interesting about this story is that we see one of the essential elements of Angel Magic: the use of a rod or weapon to control a spirit. This legend, along with the similar tales about Merlin and other wizards suggests that the belief in Angel Magic was not eradicated, but merely pushed into the background.

More evidence for the survival of Angel Magic in the dark ages is a curious eleventh century manuscript in the Nationalbibliothek Wien (Codex 1761). It presents an extremely degenerate alphabet of Hebrew letters that could only have been transmitted through numerous copyings. This indicates that the manuscript is probably a survival of material that was maintained somewhere in Europe. This likelihood is also increased by the fact that the manuscript includes an alphabet of Celtic runes, something that would definitely not have been included in an Arabic manuscript. (The alphabets from this manuscript are included in the Appendix.) The manuscript also contains a number of interesting talismans that are made of letters connected together to form a single seal or monogram. For example, the talisman in Figure 14 is described as being sacred to the crucifixion and to be able to make peace between enemies. This kind of monogram talisman is similar to the traditional altar cross found in many Catholic and Episcopal churches, where the cross is formed by the Greek letters for "Christ."

This eleventh century manuscript illustrates that some of the basic elements of Angel Magic survived in western Europe despite repeated persecutions. However, it is also highly unusual and does not represent the mainstream of European culture. Instead, one might think of western Europe as fertile ground where the seeds of Angel Magic, once replanted, could grow quickly in interest and popularity.

FIGURE 14. MEDIEVAL MONOGRAM TALISMAN[2]

FIGURE 15. ANGELS FROM 8TH CENTURY PERSIAN MANUSCRIPT[3]

ISLAMIC ANGEL MAGIC

The Angel Magic of the Hebrews and the Gnostics survived virtually unchanged within the Islamic empire. Angel Magic probably survived there because the original Chaldean rituals had originated there and the memory of Angel Magic was deep in the folklore of the people. In addition, the persecutions against Angel Magic had been less pronounced in this part of the world. A description of the magical texts in the library of Babylon in the tenth century states that treatises on Angel Magic were "innumerable," and contained, "the Ineffable name and other similar mysterious names of Angels...books with these terrible, awe-inspiring names and seals which have had that dreaded effect upon the uncalled, and from the use of which our ancestors shrunk, lest they be punished for incautious use."[4]

The Islamic Angel Magi added to the paraphernalia of Angel Magic. They popularized the magical square and invented talismans based upon it.[5] They also proliferated the use of planetary characters—sets of seven magical names, each sacred to a planet and each coded* into a magical alphabet. These characters appear frequently in medieval grimoires in Europe and in the Middle East. The amount of degeneracy, however, in the European examples suggests that some of the characters had already undergone significant alteration.

The Islamic empire not only preserved the ritual of Angel Magic, but exported it to the regions of the world that it conquered. Angel Magic literature spread throughout North Africa and into Spain. The effect of this dissemination can be gauged by the fact that one Islamic prince collected in his Spanish palace a total of 60,000 volumes.[6] It is highly likely

---

* Substituting a letter from the magical alphabet for the corresponding letter in the real alphabet.

that a library of this size contained many examples of the Angel Magic treatises that were "innumerable" in the main library at Babylon.

Not surprisingly, Spain quickly became a center in Europe for the study of the "forbidden arts," which at that time included mathematics, astrology, alchemy and Angel Magic. It is at this time that the Gnostic and Hebraic material preserved in the Islamic texts began to disseminate into the rest of Europe. The first Latin translations of Arabic and Aramaic magical texts were executed in the tenth through twelfth centuries by Spanish Jews and members of the Catholic clergy from Spain, Italy and France. At least one Latin medieval grimoire, the *Picatrix*, survives in the original Arabic, although there are many textual differences.[7]

This spread of ancient rituals of Angel Magic into Christian tradition may have begun as early as the tenth century. In 967, a young Italian monk named Gerbert journeyed to Spain, and there compiled a library which included Arabic mathematics, geometry, and astrology,[8] all closely related to Angel Magic. Gerbert is credited with introducing Arabic numerals into Christian Europe, as well as the use of clocks. It is likely that Gerbert encountered Arabic manuscripts on Angel Magic at this time and may have copied some of them.

A number of interesting rumors began to float around the enterprising young scholar. Gerbert is said to have constructed a brazen head, which would answer when it was spoken to, and thus resolve many difficult questions. Through this Angelic oracle, he was believed to have made various discoveries of hidden treasures, and to have produced visions of a magical underground palace. His learning appears to have done his career good, for he was appointed Archbishop of Rheims at an early age. He afterward became a favorite of Holy Roman Emperor Otho the Third and through Otho's influence he became archbishop of Ravenna, and finally Pope in 999, taking the name of Sylvester the Second.

As the story goes, Gerbert was habitually waited on by Angels, and that it was by their aid that he obtained the papal crown.[9] His enemies claimed that he had sold his soul to the devil, who faithfully promised him that he should live until he had celebrated high mass at Jerusalem. Gerbert actually did die shortly after officially dispensing the sacrament at the church of the Holy Cross in Jerusalem, one of the seven districts of the city of Rome. This event occurred in the year 1003.[10] A few years after Gerbert's death, one Cardinal Beno claimed that Gerbert had conversed with demons and had taught this art to his successors.[11]

One of Gerbert's successors, Gregory VII, was also reputed to be an Angel Magus. He was one of the great champions of the church and established the law of the celibacy of the clergy. Not surprisingly, Gregory was known to be particularly severe and inflexible. It is further said that Gregory was so expert in the arts of Magic, that he would throw out lightning by shaking his arm, and dart thunder from his sleeve.

It is interesting and possibly significant that popular folklore connects Popes with the practice of Angel Magic. In fact, Angel Magic was beginning to get very popular within the church. It is just after this time that there are definite signs of the influx of Angel Magic texts into the rest of Europe. It was at the beginning of the eleventh century that the Gnostic heresy reappeared in Italy,[12] and stories about Angel Magic began to spring up in Italy and France, the two countries nearest to Islamic-influenced Spain. Here is an eyewitness account of an Angel Magic ceremony in eleventh century France:

> *Everyone carrying a light in his hand, they chanted the names of demons until suddenly they saw descend among them a demon in the likeness of some sort of beast.*[13]

MEDIEVAL ANGEL MAGIC

By the end of the twelfth century, a multitude of Latin grimoires were circulating in Europe. Among them were probably early versions of the *Key of Solomon*, the *Lemegeton* and the *Sepher Raziel*. The practice of Angel Magic became common among the Catholic clergy as in France around 1169, when a priest was accused of consulting an astrologer and, with him summoning a demon.[14]

Predictably, the rediscovery of these rituals had considerable impact upon the theological attitudes of the time. The more conservative members of the clergy tended to be skeptical toward a ritual system that professed to give a priest control over Angels; however, the more radical and experimental members of the clergy embraced the grimoires as fragments of Hebrew teachings, perhaps on a par with the Old Testament itself.

The new breed of clerical Angel Magi were not satisfied with the old rituals. In accordance with the spirit of the times, they adapted and changed the rituals to make them fit more fully into the Catholic religious system as well as the social order of the period. For example, the grimoire entitled the *Lemegeton* is an Arabic ritual system that was adapted to the culture of western Europe. In comparatively unchanged ritual texts such as the *Key of Solomon*, the spirits which the magician conjures remained unnamed. In the *Lemegeton*, on the other hand, the spirits are not only named, but are given royal rank and their own personal seals that resemble miniature coats-of-arms (See Figure 16). The idea of kingly demons commanding legions of lesser spirits appealed to the medieval conception of political order.

FIGURE 16. SIGIL OF PADIEL FROM THE LEMEGETON[15]

Other elements in the *Lemegeton* are by contrast extremely ancient, such as the arrangement of the spirits into seven planetary groups,[16] and the similarity of the conjurations to those found in more Hebraic ritual systems:

> *And by this ineffable name TETRAGRAMMATON JEHOVAH, I do command thee, at which being heard the elements are overthrown, the air is shaken, the sea runneth back, the fire is quenched, the earth trembleth, and all the hosts of the celestials, terrestrials, and infernals do tremble together, and are troubled and confounded.... Wherefore come thou visibly, peaceably, and affably, now without delay, to manifest that which I desire, speaking with a clear and perfect voice.[17]*

The effect of further Christianization, however, can clearly be seen in an incantation from a later version of the *Lemegeton* excerpted in Reginald Scot's *Discoverie of Witchcraft* in 1584:

*Oh father omnipotent, oh wise sonne, oh Holie-ghost, the
searcher of harts, oh you three in person, one true god-head
in substance... by these holie names of thy sonne, to wit
ALPHA and OMEGA and all other his names, grant me
thy virtue and power, that I may be able to sit before me thy
spirits which were thrown down from heaven.*[18]

Note that despite the thousands of years separating this Christianized conjuration from its Chaldean roots, the key premise of Angel
Magic—that the name of the higher god gives power over lesser entities—remains unchanged. In fact, both the basic concept of Angel
Magic and certain ceremonial paraphernalia have survived centuries
intact while most other forms of theological belief and superstition of
comparable antiquity are merely dust.

Regardless of the attempts to Christianize Angel Magic, the conservative elements of the church objected to it. This was not because they
questioned its reality, but because they considered it unethical, for a
variety of reasons. It was a period of extreme anti-Semitism and anything Jewish was automatically suspect. Angel Magic had definite
Hebraic elements within it and thus automatically was considered
dangerous. The grimoires possessed elements of Gnosticism that
smacked of heresy even at that late date. The ability to control spirits
was still considered part of the powers of the pagan sorcerers of legend
rather than something legitimately Christian. The Templars' occupa-
tion of Palestine had given them access to the libraries of the Islamic
empire.[19] As a result, they were associated with Angel Magic and when
the Templars were persecuted, Angel Magic seemed even more disreputable. Imitation grimoires began to appear which included elements
such as black masses and human sacrifices that weren't present in the
original grimoires.

FIGURE 17. MEDIEVAL ANGELS AND DEMONS[20]

It was guilt by association. The established Catholic clergy concluded that Angel Magic was merely a tool of the devil, worthy only
of inquisition and persecution. The rebirth of Angel Magic ended in
the same way that the ancient Gnostic practices had ended—with
persecutions and death. By the beginning of the fourteenth century,
the established church had decided that the practice of Angel Magic
was plainly heretical. The Templar estates were seized and their members tried.[21] At the same time, the church cracked down on Angel
Magic. In 1318, Pope John XXII issued a Bull condemning eight Italian priests:

> *"[They] have entangled and enmeshed themselves in the*
> *dark toils of nigromancy, geomancy, and other Magic arts,*
> *possessing writings and books that treat of these arts...hav-*
> *ing consecrated certain mirrors and images according to*
> *their accursed ceremonies, [they] not unseldom make use of*
> *such objects and taking their place in circles they frequently*
> *invoke evil spirits. On occasion, moreover, they enclose in*
> *mirrors, circles, or rings, devils, who may answer their*
> *inquiries concerning the past and future.... When they have*
> *evoked these foul spirits, they essay many a curious experi-*
> *ment in every branch of diabolic lore."* [22]

The Bull goes on to mention that others in the court of the Pope himself had committed similar "enormities." The fact that Angel Magic was being practiced right under the Pope's nose shows how prevalent the practice had become among the clergy.

In 1326, John XXII dealt a death blow to the practice of Angel Magic among the clergy by issuing a Bull specifically forbidding, under pain of excommunication, both Angel Magic and alchemy. [23] As a result of this, Angel Magic was nearly eradicated from the church and its dogma. Catholic exorcism rituals are a remnant of the practice which has survived because, unlike Angel Magic, they were used by the inquisitors themselves to torture accused witches.

Soon the established church was persecuting Angel Magic outside of the clergy as well. When Peter d'Abano, a reputed Angel Magus, died, the inquisitors of the Catholic church decreed that his bones should be dug up and publicly burned. Some of his friends got word of this, and saved him from the impending disgrace by removing his remains. Disappointed in this, the inquisitors proceeded to burn him in effigy. [24]

RENAISSANCE ANGEL MAGIC

From this point on, the attitude of the church was unswervingly hostile. Angel Magic did not die, however; instead it began to be associated with humanism and ushered in what might be called the golden age of Angel Magic, the Renaissance in western Europe. The idea of the all-powerful Angel Magus, embedded in the culture of the middle ages, grew stronger as scholars and philosophers began to celebrate the glories of human achievement.

Both Catholic and Protestant branches of the church tended to view the human condition as a fall from grace. Human beings were basically corrupt and contemptible. To the humanists, however, the human race possessed a powerful spark of the godhead. Angel Magic reaffirmed the essential power and dignity of the human race by making it co-equal, if not superior, to the Angels themselves.

The church continued to persecute would-be Angel Magi, whether they belonged to the church or not. Humanists who remained under clerical jurisdiction were particularly vulnerable to rumor and slander about Angel Magic.

Take, for example, John Trithemius. Born in the year 1462, he distinguished himself by his devotion to literature while still a young man. He became Abbot of Spanheim when only twenty years of age. He wrote a great number of works and left many memorials of his life, and was an avid bibliophile. When he was chosen Abbot, the library of the convent consisted of little more than forty volumes. Shortly after, under his superintendence, it grew to many hundreds of volumes. Trithemius was accused of both necromancy and commerce with Angels.

MEDIEVAL ANGEL

The principle basis of this accusation was a story that has been told that he caused the spirit of Mary of Burgundy, the late wife of the emperor Maximilian, to appear before her bereaved husband. Another was that Trithemius had written a book about how to use secret writing to communicate thoughts to someone in another place. Trithemius maintained, however, that the Steganographia merely contained the language of Angel Magic, and categorically denied all imputation of sorcery.[25] There still exists a number of magical works attributed to Trithemius, including the Magical Calendar, a curious work that includes all the various magical correspondences of the elements, numbers, planets, and constellations.[26]

One of the most famous Angel Magi was Henry Cornelius Agrippa. Born in the year 1486, he was one of the most celebrated men of his time, highly praised by Trithemius, Erasmus, Melancthon, and other great contemporary humanists.

Agrippa was a man of the most violent passions and temper, resulting in a number of difficulties in his life. Despite this, he had a great reputation as an astrologer and an alchemist, and was believed to have possessed the philosopher's stone,* which he can't have used very often, because he was without money, subject to great persecutions, and repeatedly imprisoned. After a stormy life of triumphs and defeats, he died at the comparatively early age of forty-eight years.

Many extraordinary stories have been told of Agrippa's skills in Angel Magic. As one tale goes, Agrippa always kept a spirit attendant upon him, who accompanied him in all his travels in the shape of a black dog. When he lay on his death bed, he was earnestly pressured to repent of his sins. Being convinced of the wisdom of this, Agrippa took hold of the dog and removed a collar studded with nails, which

---

* The end product of alchemy, the philosopher's stone, is a magical substance which can transmute "base" metals (like lead) into gold.

formed a necromantic inscription. Agrippa said to the dog: "Begone, wretched animal, which hast been the cause of my entire destruction." The dog immediately ran away and plunged itself in the river, after which it was seen no more.[27]

This story is denied by Wierus, Agrippa's student, who writes that Agrippa's dog was a perfectly innocent animal that Weirus himself had often taken for walks. The sole foundation for the story lay in the fact that Agrippa had been very attached to the dog, which ate at the table and slept in the same bed as its master. Weirus further remarks that Agrippa was accustomed to remain in his room for as much as a week at a time. People wondered how he could have such accurate information of what was going on in all parts of the world. Lacking any better explanation, they assumed that his intelligence was communicated to him by his dog. Weirus points out, however, that Agrippa had correspondents in every quarter of the globe, and received letters from them daily, and that this was the real source of his extraordinary intelligence.[28]

According to another story, Agrippa had occasion one time to be absent for a few days from his residence at Louvain. During his absence he entrusted his wife with the key to his Museum, telling her that nobody should be allowed to enter. Agrippa happened at that time to have a boarder in his house, a young fellow of insatiable curiosity, who pestered his hostess, until at length he obtained the forbidden key. The first thing in the Museum that attracted his attention was a book of spells and incantations. He spread this book upon a desk and began to read aloud. He had not long done this, when a knock was heard at the door of the chamber. The youth took no notice, but continued reading. Presently there was a second knock, which somewhat alarmed the young man. A minute later, the door opened and a devil entered. "For what purpose have I been called?" asked the spirit. When the student made no answer, the devil advanced towards him, seized him by the throat, and strangled him, indignant that his presence should thus be invoked from mere presumption.

The story of the student who obtains access to the magician's workbooks is common in folklore.* The idea of stealing magical power is attractive, because it appeals to our natural sense of laziness. Why study for years when we can merely rifle the workbooks of an experienced Magus? The tales also consistently point out the danger inherent in this practice.

Angel Magi were seen as superhuman—able to control vast powers, learn secret information, and obtain whatever they wanted through the power of the Angels that they conjured. The enemies of the Angel Magi naturally believed these Angels to be devils in disguise. The Angel Magi themselves, however, always maintained that Angel Magic was intended to be heavenly and that they would never stoop to conjure devils.

Agrippa's main claim to fame as an Angel Magus was his *De Occulta Philosophia*, a compilation from many sources that serves virtually as an encyclopedia of occult lore. *De Occulta Philosophia* (Concerning Occult Philosophy) provided the entire philosophical framework for Angel Magic of the time, without actually providing the rituals to accomplish it. It was written around 1510, but not published until 1533, about a year before Agrippa's death. The publication created an uproar in scholarly circles, because for the first time the conceptual framework of Angel Magic was made available to large numbers of people and there was a wild upsurge of interest in the subject.

De Occulta Philosophia was followed by numerous other occult publications, many of which contained Angel Magic rituals of greater or lesser antiquity. Probably the most widely distributed was a small

---

*As in "The Sorcerer's Apprentice" segment of the Disney movie, *Fantasia*.

book containing what purported to be a final chapter to *De Occulta Philosophia*. This book, published in 1565, supposedly provided the keys to actually performing the Angel Magic ceremonies that the main body of *De Occulta Philosophia* only hints at. It was published along with another curious work entitled the *Heptameron*, attributed to Peter d'Abano (Peter of Apono). While the actual authorship of both works is questionable, there's little doubt that the works proceed from the same kind of thinking that lies behind Agrippa's work.

The figure of the Angel Magus became increasingly common in the literature of the period. Often literary descriptions of Angel Magi were surprisingly detailed as in this list of the various equipment that Angel Magi use in their ceremonies:

> *halowed chalke, water and palme, circle pentacles, and plates used for fense, crowne, swords, and scepter, as a token of power, fire, oyles, and powders to make fumagacions, tedious fastes, wasshinges and shavings, of the consecration, of their invocations, constructions, ligacions, maledictiones and other forsaid instrumentes....*[29]

Manuscripts and books on Angel Magic began to be widely circulated. By 1584, one author was able to complain that:

> *Conjurors carrie about at this daie, bookes intitled under the names of Adam, Abel, Tobie, and Enoch; which Enoch they repute the most divine fellow in such matters.*[30]

Ten years later, the literature of Angel Magic had become so well known to the public at large that the playwright Christopher Marlowe actually included a satire—in Latin no less, and translated here—of an Angel Magic ritual inside his highly popular play *Doctor Faustus*:

Be propitious to me, gods of Acheron! May the triple name of Jehovah prevail! Spirits of fire, air water, hail! Prince of the East, Beelzebub, monarch of burning hell, and Demogorgon, we propitiate you so that Mephostophilis may appear and rise! Why do you delay? By Jehovah, by Gehenna, and by the holy water that I now sprinkle, and by the sign of the cross which I now make, and by our prayers, let Mephostophilis now arise, summoned by us! Return, Mephostophilis, in the image of a friar.[31]

Marlowe's original sources were probably the fourth book of *De Occulta Philosophia* and the *Heptameron*. However, Marlowe changed the conjurations so that they became diabolical rather than Angelic. Marlowe made Faustus into a black Angel Magus because for some unknown reason he wanted to slander Doctor John Dee, probably the greatest Angel Magus of all time. The life and career of John Dee represents a high point in this history of Angel Magic and provides the root source for much of the Angel Magic that is practiced today. Because of this, we'll be examining John Dee's work specifically in the next few chapters.

THE HOLY WOMEN AT THE SEPULCHRE

The Making of
an Angel Magus

o far, we've looked at the practice of Angel Magic in ancient times and we've traced its heritage through the ages. We've seen that there are elements of the traditional Angel Magic rituals that are very old indeed. We've also seen that Angel Magic has continued to evolve to match the different requirements and theologies of the cultures which have adopted it. Some questions remain unanswered, however: Where does Angel Magic come from? Why are there so many different rituals and recipes? Is Angel Magic useful? How do Angel Magi benefit from its practice? The best way to answer these questions is to examine the life and work of Doctor John Dee.

Unlike the other Angel Magi, of whom little is known (especially about their magical practices) there is so much information about John Dee that it is difficult to fit all the pieces into the together. Dee was a rabid diarist, recording nearly every aspect of his life in multiple journals. Not only have many of his diaries survived, but many of his letters have been preserved in different collections. Furthermore, he was an extremely conspicuous figure in the late sixteenth century, and many famous people have left records of their interactions with him.

John Dee was very different from the Angel Magi that came before him in that he was brave enough to let the world know what he was attempting. Unlike Agrippa and Trithemius, both of whom denied having practiced the art, Dee openly and fully declared that he was an Angel Magus and made no apologies for the fact. He was patronized by a number of very powerful people, including Queen Elizabeth, Count Albert Lasky of Poland, King Stephen of Poland (briefly), Count Rosenberg of Trebona, and Sir Walter Raleigh. Rather than being at odds with the authorities, Dee was at one point given the equivalent of a government grant to pursue "scientific" research into Angel Magic.

By studying John Dee, we learn about the inner mechanics of Angel Magic and the motivations of the Angel Magi. In this way we can reach a deeper understanding of this interesting and ancient art.

◠◡

THE EARLY YEARS

John Dee's Angel Magic was a natural outgrowth of his interest in nature and what we would today call science. He was born in London in the year 1527, the son of a gentleman servitor of King Henry VIII. Royal courts in those times employed a large number of servitors and courtiers who performed roles which could be somewhat servile, such as emptying the royal chamberpot, or exalted, such as escorting and entertaining high-ranking ambassadors from foreign lands.[1]

These gentlemen servitors often had their families with them in London, sometimes even living in the palace. By the time Dee was born, Henry VIII was already old. The king had always shown a preference to favor and advance the careers of young men who reminded him of himself at a younger age. "Young King Hal" had been highly athletic. Two of his greatest loves in life, not including women, had been jousting and hunting. In light of this, it is unlikely that the young John Dee was very popular at Henry's court. Dee was bookish in the extreme.

Dee was forever wrapped up in some arcane text or studying some obscure subject. Perhaps it is not surprising, then, that he left the court for Cambridge at the tender age of fifteen. His behavior at Cambridge reveals the level of his dedication to learning. For several years he allowed himself only four hours a sleep a day, spending the rest of his time studying and occasionally attending church.

He must have seemed a very unusual person to the rough and tumble scholars of Elizabethan Cambridge. Dee clearly had little time for the drinking and wenching that were the customary behaviors of the student body.* He worked hard, and as a result, accumulated a great deal of learning in a very short time. We can also assume that due to the rigors of his schedule he made few friends. In any case, his talents were not appreciated at Cambridge. At one point, while superintending the exhibition of a Greek play of Aristophanes, he built an artificial scarab, or beetle, which flew up to the palace of Jupiter, with a man and a basket of provisions on its back. This bit of cleverness was to haunt John Dee for the rest of his life.

Dee's stagecraft may seem trivial today, but the special effects of the modern cinema have left us jaded. This was not the case in the mid-sixteenth century. Audiences were unsophisticated. Stage plays

---

* Some things never change.

had only the simplest of props. Dee's audience had never seen anything like his flying scarab before. Rather than assuming that it was simply done with wires and mirrors, Dee's contemporaries believed that he must have used some form of Angel Magic to accomplish this unheard-of feat.

Even though it was thirty years before he took up the practice of Angel Magic seriously, Dee was already a wizard in the minds of his contemporaries. He was never able to shed this judgment, and perhapt it may have influenced Dee to actually take up the practice of Angel Magic. Having been accused of it so long, he may have concluded that he might as well be guilty in earnest.

THE CELEBRATED SCHOLAR

The flying scarab incident made Dee even less popular at Cambridge, and he did not stay there long. Dee had been translating the works of Euclid and was asked to lecture on the subject at the University of Louvaine. Probably to Dee's surprise, his lectures were extremely well-received. His work had been virtually ignored at Cambridge, but it quickly attracted the attention of the dukes of Mantua and Medina. Dee traveled on to Paris where his lectures were instantly popular. Students crowded around the doors of the University to hear him speak.

Today, it is difficult for us to imagine how a series of lectures on Euclid could have generated so much interest. We tend to think of scholars and scholarly research as bone-dry boring, but in Dee's time people got excited about ideas, and students were fully capable of fighting and even killing each other during arguments about religion and philosophy.

Dee's views of Euclid received massive attention because they were revolutionary. Dee used Euclid's work to explain that all branches of learning and the sciences are interrelated and tied together by mathematics.[2] This was a very different viewpoint than that of the Medieval church, which tended to believe that divine knowledge was separate from secular knowledge. The traditional view held that theology was revealed truth and that secular science* was somehow suspect. Dee's idea made it possible to combine theology and science into a complete and integrated system.

When Dee returned to England from his triumphs in Paris, he found himself to be something of a celebrity. He was received by young King Edward (Henry having died), who was so impressed with Dee that he awarded him a pension of one hundred crowns per year.† The awarding of this pension was royal recognition that Dee was considered the greatest scholar in the England of his time.

It is likely at this time that Dee met the then-princess Elizabeth, if indeed he had not met her when he was a young boy. She was only a few years younger than Dee, attractively nubile and very studious. If they met at this age, it is possible that Dee developed a crush on the young princess. Or perhaps it was the other way around. In any case, there was an undeniable affection between the two of them that lasted the whole of their long lives.

This brings up an interesting question. Could Dee, in the back of his mind, have once entertained the notion of marrying Elizabeth? This is not as far-fetched as it seems. At the time, Elizabeth was considered a bastard unlikely to ever ascend to the throne and Dee had

---

* The term "science" was not used in Dee's time. I use it here because it best approximates the concept of knowledge that is not part of theological speculation.

† To put this into perspective, an entire family could live quite well on a fraction of this amount.

some traces of royal blood in him. Whatever the case, Elizabeth never abandoned Dee over the long period of their association—even when he became unpopular with her subjects—and Dee never abandoned Elizabeth, considering her his ultimate patron, even when he was traveling far abroad.

Still, the days of Queen Elizabeth's reign were far away. King Edward did not live long and was succeeded, not by Elizabeth, but by Mary, the daughter of Henry's first wife. At first, the change of royalty did not affect Dee; however, when Mary committed herself to the suppression of the Protestant heresy, Dee's work immediately fell under suspicion. Dee was caught writing letters to Elizabeth's servants and soon found himself imprisoned on charges of trying to kill Queen Mary through the use of enchantment.

Dee was eventually cleared of heresy, and the experience did not appear to have greatly affected his dedication to learning, because he soon afterwards presented a petition to the Queen, requesting her cooperation in a plan for preserving and recovering certain monuments of classical antiquity.

One of Dee's main interests at this time was astrology. When Mary died and Elizabeth ascended the throne, her favorite, Robert Dudley, commissioned Dee to select the most auspicious day for her coronation. This was just the first of many indications of Elizabeth's friendship toward Dee. In 1571, when Dee was ill in France, Elizabeth sent two of her personal physicians to help him get better. She also visited him at his home in Mortlack, where she enjoyed examining his library and the scientific instruments and curiosities that he had collected over the years.

Dee flourished under Elizabeth's patronage. He collected an enormous library of five thousand books and manuscripts, a collection that makes up the core of today's British Library. He delved into navigation and geography, and used historical research to defend Elizabeth's claim to be the ruler of various parts of the globe, such as Iceland. A number of emperors and princes offered him patronage, which he refused, being happy in Elizabeth's service. The Russian Czar offered Dee two thousand pounds a year if he would move to Moscow. He was the most respected scholar of his day, basking in the attention of a Queen who thought highly of him and treated him as one of the treasures of her realm.

FIGURE 18. DOCTOR JOHN DEE[3]

THE MAGIC BEGINS

When Dee approached his fifties, however, he was seized by a strange malaise. Today, I suppose we would have said that he had a mid-life crisis. He became dissatisfied with all that he had learned. He wanted to discover the secrets of nature, the philosopher's stone, and the elixir of life. He wanted to build machines that could fly through the air or beneath the sea. He wanted to be able to communicate with people immediately, even though they were many miles away. In short, Dee wanted to bring into the world all the technological marvels that we take for granted today. It was this quest for what he called "radical knowledge" that brought Dee to the practice of Angel Magic.

The notion that technological breakthroughs could result from communicating with Angels seems odd to the modern mind. To Dee, however, the concept had all the force of logic. Dee, unlike a modern scientist, did not see human knowledge as something that was growing and changing as people learned more and more about the universe. Dee and his contemporaries didn't think of human history in term of progress, but in terms of rediscovery.

The men and women of the Renaissance were in awe of the majesty of the past. They looked back at the glorious ruins and literature of Egypt, Greece, and Rome and compared them unfavorably with the products of their contemporary culture. Dee considered Adam—the first human—to be the perfect scientist, the ultimate repository of all human wisdom. Furthermore, Dee had a deep respect for the prophets of the Old Testament, who had received knowledge directly from God or indirectly through intermediary Angels. Because Dee believed that all knowledge existed in its purest form inside the mind of God, Angel Magic seemed a convenient method for extracting that knowledge. In short, Dee thought that he could use Angel Magic to reestablish the power and wisdom that the ancients had so obviously possessed.

Having committed himself to the practice of Angel Magic, Dee obtained a number of different stones and crystals for this purpose. Using these stones, the observer could hold conversations, ask questions and receive answers from the Angels that appeared in the mirror. Two of Dee's stones can be seen today in the British Museum: a black onyx mirror about eight inches across, and a crystal ball of about two inches in diameter. Based upon his diary, it is likely that he used a number of other stones as well.

Dee's records of his first experiments still survive. Working with a scryer named Saul on December 22, 1581, Dee conjured the Angel Anael into a "Christaline Globe."

> *Saul, looking into my stone to spy Anael, saw one which answered to that name. But being earnestly requested to tell the truth if he really were Anael, another did appear, very beautiful, with yellow apparrel that glittered like gold. He had star beams blazing and spreading from his eyes. He wrote in the stone many Hebrew letters of transparent gold, which Saul was not able to read, so that I could not write them down. A bright star did go right down by him and many other visions appeared...*[4]

A conversation then resulted between Dee and Anael, conducted partly in Latin, partly in English, with a few smatterings of Hebrew. At the end of the session, Dee notes that the bright Angel was actually named Annael (rather than Anael) and that the Angel declared himself to be sacred to the planet Venus. This session is interesting not only because it is the earliest in Dee's records, but it is also shows that

Dee was perfectly capable of getting impressive results without his most famous scryer Edward Kelly. In fact, it is difficult to find major differences between Dee's scrying session with Kelly and those with other scryers. However, we have far more records of Kelly's scrying than of any of the others.

During these ceremonies, the Angels would sometimes show themselves on the surface of the stone, and sometimes in different parts of the room by virtue of the action of the stone. Only the scryer could see the Angels and hear their voices, and was required to have his eyes and his ears thus engaged throughout the ceremony. This meant that there had to be two people present: the scryer and the someone to read the prayers and incantations and write down what the scryer dictated.

Edward Talbot replaced Saul as Dee's scryer, although in Dee's diaries it is not exactly clear whether Edward Talbot was actually someone else, or Edward Kelly under an assumed name. Elias Ashmole, who preserved and copied most of Dee's manuscripts, suggests that Talbot and Kelly may have been different people. Ashmole notes in his copy of Dee's magical diary:

> E. T. was unwilling to serve as scryer any further because Michael willed him to marry and it is probable that he left after... Talbot went away from Mortlack and deserted his employment.... Kelly had been employed as scryer sometime before the said falling out.[5]

In any case, the name Talbot soon disappeared from the diaries. Dee settled down into a productive period of Angel Magic with Edward Kelly, who was to become the most famous of his scryers.

Edward Kelly remains something of an enigma. We see him only through Dee's eyes and have no other record of his experiences. History has cast him in the role of a charlatan who preyed upon the credulous Dee. This view is oversimplistic.

A number of unsavory rumors have clung to Kelly over the years. According to one source, when he was a young man he was accused of forgery, brought to trial, convicted, and lost his ears in the pillory. The truth of this story has been questioned on the grounds that he would never have been received at the court of the German Emperor, as he was some years later, had he suffered this mutilation. Another persistent rumor is that prior to being employed by Dee, he had dug up a corpse and used incantations to cause it to answer questions and predict future events. This is probably just an item of folklore that has attached itself to Kelly. No eyewitness accounts of such an event seem to have survived.

Dee's diary reveals Kelly to be a highly colorful personality. Extremely charming when he wanted to be, he also had a violent streak and was often unpredictable in his daily behavior. He frequently threatened to leave Dee, usually on the grounds that he believed Dee's Angels were actually devils in disguise.

Whatever Kelly's true nature, he was, by all accounts, very different from Dee. Dee was a gentleman with an unspotted life, honored by royalty. Kelly was at the very least somewhat of a scoundrel. Despite this, it is clear from Dee's records that their relationship was much more than that of master and servant. Dee shows an undeniable affection and concern for Kelly's welfare, while Kelly frequently protests his friendship and loyalty to Dee. The two of them got along tolerably well and had a very close association that lasted many years. They experienced numerous adventures and troubles together, and through it all maintained a reasonable level of camaraderie and friendship.

One of the first things that Dee and Kelly attempted together was an exploratory journey to the celebrated ruins of Glastonbury Abbey in Somersetshire. Here they believed that they had, by accident, located a small vial of the fabled "elixir of life"—the precious alchemical substance said to cure all diseases, prolong life, and turn lead into silver or gold. The vial was supposed to have dated from the time of Saint Dunstan in the tenth century.[6] While they were exceedingly pleased at this discovery, they didn't discover how to use the substance for some time afterwards.

Dee and Kelly continued their experiments for years, conjuring various Angels into stones and recording their actions and utterances. Dee's diaries reveal that the Angels with whom they spoke were arranged into a complex hierarchy, with lesser Angels on the bottom and the more powerful Angels on the top. It required a different set of ceremonies and sigils to conjure and control the Angels at each level, the formula for which could only be obtained from the Angels at the next level down. It was like a complicated bureaucracy, where the Magus had to learn and master the lesser officials before he could be admitted to the presence of the greater and more powerful officials.

At first, Dee employed rituals from an unidentified Magical text, probably something adapted from the fourth book of *De Occulta Philosophia*. As the workings continued, this basic system was embellished both by Dee's cabalistic elaborations and by magical material dictated by the Angels. Dee was an Anglican with Catholic leanings, and his Christianity is revealed in the many prayers that occur during the communications. Dee undoubtedly perceived his ritual system as holy rather than profane. Nevertheless, Dee's ritual system was without some of the trappings usually associated with Christianized Angel Magic: There was no performance of the Mass, and there is no record of a Magical circle.

The rituals began with Dee and the scryer sitting at a table, separated from the floor by cabalistic tablets upon which a complex series of acrostic designs had been written. After a few preliminary prayers, the scryer would gaze into a crystal while Dee recorded what the scryer saw.

Through this process, the Angels first revealed a new system of Magic, sacred to the Angels of the seven planets. This system, which Dee called the "Mystical Heptarchy" was only a prelude to the more fully-realized and complete system of Enochian Angel Magic for which Dee is most famous.

VOYAGE TO CRACOW

While still in England, Dee and Kelly were visited by Albert Lasky, a Polish nobleman, Lord Palatine of the principality of Siradia. Lasky came to England to acquaint himself with the glories of the reign of Elizabeth. The queen and her favorite, the Earl of Leicester, received Lasky with every courtesy and attention. Having shown him all the wonders of her court at Westminster and Greenwich, she sent him to Oxford, with a command to the heads of colleges to pay him every attention. Lasky, however, was disappointed at what he found there, and instead wanted to meet the famous Doctor Dee.

Leicester was only too happy to comply and brought Lasky to Mortlack by sailing up the Thames on Elizabeth's private barge. Lasky was fascinated by Dee and even more fascinated by what he could learn about Dee's experiments. After two or three interviews, Lasky convinced Dee to admit him as a third party to their Angel Magic rituals, from which the rest of the world had been carefully excluded. Lasky offered Dee his patronage, if Dee would move to Lasky's territory inside of Poland.

Dee at first was hesitant. While he was beginning to feel that he had a number of enemies at Elizabeth's court, he was not at a time in his life when it would be easy to move away from his home and the connections and friendships of a lifetime. The Angels, however, were fond of Lasky. They told Dee that Lasky should shortly become king of Poland and several other kingdoms, that he should overcome many armies of Saracens and Pagans, and prove a mighty conqueror. The Angels insisted and Dee finally caved in.

Despite the Angels' confidence, Lasky had a somewhat questionable character. While he was certainly intelligent, he was not particularly reliable. He possessed extensive lands in Poland, but still had to borrow money to make ends meet during his trip. Some of these debts he failed to pay before leaving England. The first time that Dee had reason to question his decision to accept Lasky's patronage happened as soon as they crossed the English channel. Lasky, lacking the funds to support Dee's entourage, quickly rented a carriage for himself and his servant and merely instructed Dee and his party to follow as quickly as they could. Luckily, Elizabeth had given Dee a present of some money before they left, which allowed Dee, Kelly, their wives, and servants to make the journey at Dee's own expense.

The trip was neither easy nor pleasant. At one point, the rigging in Dee's ship became entangled and they collided with another ship, almost capsizing the both of them. At another point, the party was forced to cross a river on the ice because the bridge had fallen down. They finally ended up in Cracow, where Lasky kept a house. There, Dee and Kelly spent a great deal of time in alchemical experiments, trying to discover the usage of the elixir that they had found at Glastonbury.

They also conducted many Angel Magic ceremonies with Lasky present. The Angels made many predictions of wealth, fame, and glory for their patron. None of these predictions came true, however, and Lasky soon began to tire of the endless string of unfulfilled promises. Not so Dee. He was more fascinated than ever by the Angelic communications, especially since they had entered an entirely new stage. They had begun to reveal Enochian Angel Magic, today reputed to be the most powerful ever revealed to mankind.

Jacob's Ladder

5

The
Angelic Keys

uring one of their Angel Magic ceremonies in Cracow, Kelly told Dee that the Angels were tapping out letters on a magic square.

> *[The angel] hath a rod or wand in his hand...it is of Gold ...He standeth upon his round table of Christal or rather Mother of Pearl: There appear an infinite number of letters on the same, as thick as can stand by another...He standeth and pointeth with his rod to the letters of his Table, as if he made some account or reckoning.*[1]

This had happened once before in England, resulting in a gigantic collection of mysterious tables that the Angels attributed to the prophet Enoch. Dee at first thought that they were about to receive more of the same, but he was pleasantly surprised. Rather than complex tables, the Angels dictated what appeared to be a set of conjurations in a foreign language which Dee—although a consummate linguist—had never seen before.

THE ANGELIC LANGUAGE*

Dee was asked to prepare a book in which the Angelic conjurations would be written. The procedure was laborious and difficult, and apparently confusing to both Dee and Kelly. Nevertheless, they continued to record this bizarre information, eventually receiving an entire collection. Accompanying the conjurations were a number of magical squares said to be of vast potency, a hierarchical arrangement of spirits who reportedly understood the conjurations, and the names of thirty "Aires," or "planes of existence" in which the Angels were said to "dwell."

The strange language was called, somewhat unimaginatively, "Angelic." The Angels told Dee that it was the original language that Adam had spoken in the garden of Eden and that Hebrew was merely a degenerate form of it. This made Dee very excited because he knew that divine names control Angels, and the most powerful conjurations always contained Hebrew words, or at least words that sounded like Hebrew. Take, for example, this conjuration from the grimoires the *Key of Solomon*:

> *Sceaboles arbaron elohi elimigith herenobulcule methe baluth timayal villaquiel teveni yevie, ferete bachuhaba guvarin... Almiras cheros maitor tangedem transidim suvantos baelaios bored belamith castumi dabuel...Saturiel harchiel daniel beneil assimonem...Metatron melekh beroth noth venibbeth mach.*[2†]

---

* A condensed version of this chapter appeared in my earlier work *The Enochian Magick of Doctor John Dee*. This version differs in that it provides more detail and represents a more balanced account of the possible sources for the Angelic language.

† I've formatted and excerpted the Solomonic material to emphasize the similarity.

While the Hebrew in the conjuration is doggerel, it contains some words that are recognizable: "elohi," "Saturiel," and "melekh," however, there had been so many copyist errors that the original conjuration has become indecipherable. The same was true in Dee's day.

Dee's "discovery" of Angelic filled him with excitement because it meant he could restore the conjurations of Angel Magic to their original and most powerful form. Because the Angelic language was supposed to be the purest form of language—the very language with which Adam conversed with God—Dee felt certain that he could use it to control the very highest Angels in the heavenly hierarchy.

The Angelic language was conveniently dictated in the form of a set of conjurations. The Angels called these conjuration "Claves" (keys)—an obvious reference to the *Key of Solomon*, illustrating the connection between the grimoires and the material that the Angels were dictating. On the surface, the Angelic keys, like the one that follows, were similar to the conjurations in the *Key of Solomon*:

Ol sonf vorsg, gohó Iad balt lansh calz vonpho, sobra z-ol ror i ta nazpsad Graa ta Malprg ds hol-q Qäa nothóa zimz Od commah ta nobloh zien: Soba thil gnonp prge aldi Ds urbs óbóleh grsam: Casárm ohoréla cabá pir Ds zonrensg cab erm Jadnah: Pïlah farzm znrza adná gono Iádpil Ds hom tóh Soba Ipam Lu Ipāmis Ds lóhólo vep zomd Poamal od bogpa aäi ta piap piamos od vaooan ZACARe c-a od ZAMRAN odo cicle Qäá zorge, lap zirdo noco MAD Hoath Iaida.[3]

Unlike the Solomonic conjuration, the Angelic key had a complete English translation, which the Angels dictated separately. For example, the Angelic key given above translates to:

I raygne over you sayeth the God of Justice in powre exalted above the firmaments of wrath: in Whose hands the Sonne is as a sword, and the Moon as a through-thrusting fire which measureth your garments in the mydst of my vestures, and trussed you together as the palms of my hands: Whose seats I garnished with the fire of gathering, and beautified your garments with admiration, to whom I made a law to govern the holy ones, and delivered you a rod with the ark of knowledg. Moreover you lifted up your voyces and sware obedience and faith to him that liveth and triumpheth, whose beginning is not nor ende can not be, which shyneth as a flame in the myddst of your pallace and rayngneth amongst you as the ballance of righteousnes, and truth: Move therfore, and shew yourselves: open the Mysteries of your Creation: Be frendely unto me: for I am the servant of the same your God: the true Worshipper of the Highest.[4]

What is most interesting about this translation is that it bears very little resemblance to the colloquial conjurations in the grimoires. Gone are the lists of Hebraic names of God. The word YHVH does not appear at all in the Angelic Keys; instead there are curious new names for God, like *Madzilodarp* (literally "the God of stretch-forth and conquer"). Gone are the citations to Saints and the traditional Angels like Michael. Instead, there are tantalizing references to beings like "the spirits of the 4th angle" and "the thunderers of wrath and judgement."

Furthermore, the structure of the Angelic Keys are different from the structure of the grimoires. Rather than an elaborate series of alternating threats and supplications, the Angelic Keys are simple statements of the power and office of the spirits and a request that they appear. Even the name Satan is missing from the Angelic Keys, replaced by the chilling Telocvovim ("death-dragon").

It is surprising that this should appear suddenly in the milieu of a Renaissance Angel Magus, because the material is so different from the medieval grimoires available to Dee and Kelly at the time. The Heptarchical system—dictated by Kelly while still in England—was much more typical, being quite similar to the *Heptameron* of Peter d'Abano, a work that had been published nearly twenty years earlier.

The Angelic language is extremely curious for a number of other reasons as well. Angelic does not seem to be arranged to be comfortable to the human vocal system, similar to the Hebrew Cabala. Kelly said that the Angels pointed out the letters on a chart, rather than speaking the words aloud. Whether or not this is true, the Angelic language does have its own grammar and syntax. A detailed examination of the Keys reveals a number of basic grammatical rules:[5]

- Angelic words can be connected to form portmanteaux. For example, the Enochian word ZIRENAIAD meaning "I am the Lord your God" is a combination of ZIR (I am)—ENAY (lord)—IAD (God).

- Angelic nouns are declined irregularly.

- Angelic numbers are unrelated to any known numerical system. Numbers even into the thousands are expressed by unique names, as if the consciousness that used them were capable of recalling an inhumanly large vocabulary.

- Angelic verbs are irregular but can be conjugated. The two most extensive verb systems are ZIR (to be) and GOHUS (to speak).

ZIR		
Present Tense	**Past Tense**	**Negative Forms**
ZIR - I am	ZIROP - He was	IPAM - There is not
I - He is	ZIROM - There were	IPAMIS - There cannot be
Pll - She is		
Tl - It is	**Future Tense**	**Subjunctive Mood**
CHIS - We/You are	CHISO - It shall be	CHRISTEOS - Let there be
ZODCHIS - They are	TRIAN - They shall be	

FIGURE 19. CONJUGATION OF ANGELIC VERB ZIR

GOHUS		
Present tense	**Perfect Tense**	**Passive Voice**
GOHUS - I say	GOHON - They have said	GOHULIM - It is said
GOHO - He says		
GOHIA - We say	**Present Active Participle**	
	GOHOL - Saying	

FIGURE 20. CONJUGATION OF ANGELIC VERB GOHUS

What is even more interesting is that there are few internal inconsistencies within the hundreds of words that were dictated. The English versions match the Enochian almost perfectly, even though the Angelic for first four Keys were dictated backwards, which would have made it very difficult for Kelly to have composed them secretly and then dictated them from memory.

The standard reference work for the study of the Angelic language is Donald Laycock's *Complete Enochian Dictionary*. Laycock suggests that the Angelic language is English-like both in word order and in pronunciation. He gives an example where English is the only language that matches the Angelic; however, the Angelic Keys include many other passages where the Angelic phrasing makes for extremely awkward English. For example, *Niiso Crip Ip Nidali* is glossed in English as "Come away, but not your noyses." Because this is addressed to the "Thunderers of Wrath and Judgement," what is probably meant by is "leave wherever you are and come here, but don't make thundering noises." The Angelic language expresses the concept much more succinctly than the English translation. Similarly, the Angelic word *Telocvovim* glossed as "him who has fallen," but is actually a contraction of *Teloch* (death) and *Vovin* (dragon), literally "death-dragon" —a possible reference to Satan's transformation during his fall. Words like Telocvovim are much more Germanic than English. In short, the Angelic language is no more English-like than any other non-English language; the fact that there are some matches is not significant.

Laycock also states that the Angelic language has English pronunciations. Unfortunately, as the Angels' "mouthpiece," Kelly never pronounced the Angelic words. Furthermore, if Angelic letter arrangement has random characteristics, as Laycock claims, then the English-like pronunciation cannot be an inherent quality of the language itself. Far more likely is that Dee assigned pronunciations to the Angelic because he wished to speak the keys in a ceremony and, being English, adapted them as well as he could to his native tongue. Indeed, outside of few minor suggestions, the spirits seem unconcerned with pronunciation. The Angelic language in its basic form makes few concessions to the human vocal chords.

So what was going on here? A highly original form of Angel Magic suddenly appears in Dee's work, accompanied by a complex, internally-consistent foreign language. There are really only three explanations for this sudden appearance: Kelly fabricated the Keys either consciously or unconsciously; Kelly plagiarized the Keys from an otherwise unknown source; or Kelly was really receiving communications from Angelic beings. Let's look at each of these possibilities in more detail.

DID KELLY FABRICATE THE ANGELIC KEYS?

Historians have traditionally cast Kelly as a "fraud who deluded his pious master"[6] but the evidence does not justify this judgment. It is true that Kelly accepted fifty pounds per year for his services to Dee, but such annuities were the basis for survival in Elizabethan times. Far from encouraging Dee, Kelly eventually began to question the Angelic nature of the spirits, and frequently tried to extricate himself from Dee's employ. On the other hand, if Kelly had been trying to plunder Dee's money, why would he try to convince Dee that the spirits were devils? Why would Kelly lead Dee into Poland, where both Dee and Kelly and their families experienced numerous financial difficulties? If Kelly were a fraud, he could much more easily have lifted Dee's purse at Mortlack.

Furthermore, it is difficult to account for the serious stylistic differences between Kelly's usual writing style and the utterances that he attributed to the spirits. Kelly was an uninspired writer, as the following excerpt represents:

> *The heavenly cope hath in him nature's fower*
> *Two hidden, but the rest to sight appear:*
> *Wherein the spermes of all the bodies lower*
> *Most secrett are, yett spring forth once a yeare...*[7]

Contrast those stilted and awkward lines with the final Angelic Key that was dictated to Dee:

> *The work of man and his pomp, let them be defaced: His buyldings Let them become caves for the beasts of the field: Confownd her understanding with darknes. For why? It repenteth me I made Man.*[8]

It seems almost impossible that this powerful passage could have been written by the same hand, or that Kelly's own writing skill could have produced such passages of eldrich beauty as:

"Can the wings of the windes understand your voyces of wonder?...

Stronger are your fete then the barren stone:

And mightier are your voices than the manifold windes..."[9]

Admittedly, stylistic differences are subtle gauges of authorship. More concrete evidence against Kelly fabricating his visions lies in the complexity of the Enochian keys. Could Kelly, whose single linguistic accomplishment was schoolboy Latin, and whose English was laced with colloquialisms, have devised an entire language, with its own unique grammar and syntax?

It took J.R.R. Tolkien, a professor of philology, years to fabricate the Elvish tongue that figures so largely in his work. If Kelly fabricated the keys, he would have had to do so in a matter of days. In short, if Kelly was the conscious author of the Keys, then he possessed a far greater literary competence than he ever exhibited elsewhere.

This is not to say that he might not unconsciously have fabricated the Keys. After all, language is a product of the human mind. The unconscious mind is often capable of feats that are impossible to the conscious mind. There may be something to the theory that Kelly hallucinated the visions. It has been suggested that Dee may have propelled Kelly into a state of artificial psychosis with their ceremonies.[10] Kelly may also have had multiple personalities, for the spirits talk in biblical dialects quite different from his normal speech, and it seemed that Kelly was having trouble distinguishing between his own thoughts and those of the spirits. According to Dee, Kelly complained of "a great stir and moving in his brains, very sensible and distinct, as of a creature of human shape and lineaments going up and down, to and fro in his brains and within his skull."[11]

Dee was forcing Kelly to perform ceremonies on an almost daily basis, and for hours at a stretch. This might push anybody over the edge, especially if he were unstable in the first place.

From the evidence in the text, we can conclude that although Kelly may have lied or exaggerated about what he perceived, there is no direct textual evidence to suggest he was a total fraud. It is also unfair to project twentieth-century materialism onto a man who possessed an Elizabethan world view, which obviously included a belief in the existence of spirits. Kelly probably believed that he was in touch with *something*. On the other hand, a scryer's perception of a non-material being does not necessarily guarantee the objective existence of that being. If Kelly were hallucinating, his belief in the existence of the spirits would be justified, and the stylistic differences could be the result of a semi-controlled schizophrenia. As Peter French points out in his biography of Dee, the doctor's magnetic personality and complete belief in the reality of Magic experiences could have led Kelly, and the other clairvoyants, into an artificial state of psychosis. Kelly's hysterical temperament builds a strong case for the theory that, toward the close of his operations with Dee, Kelly was on the brink of insanity.

None of this overcomes the objection that the Keys are too radically different from the literature available at the time to have been created by anyone schooled in traditional Angel Magic. We are forced to look elsewhere for a more satisfying explanation.

DID KELLY PLAGIARIZE THE KEYS?

We can probably eliminate the possibility that Kelly, on all occasions, was willfully deceiving Dee; however, I feel it would be a mistake to assume that all of Kelly's visions were valid, or that everything he perceived was of major significance. On at least one occasion he lied about what he supposedly heard, presenting Dee with a singularly uninspired poem in his own literary style which he claimed had been dictated by spirits in his bedroom. In fact, as the magical operations continued, Kelly's behavior became increasingly bizarre, as if contact with a foreign intelligence was altering or destroying his sanity.

There is some compelling evidence that Kelly may have plagiarized portions of the material he dictated to Dee. Edward Kelly was a magician and alchemist in his own right. This is significant because, during the period in which the Angelic Keys were dictated, Kelly was performing ceremonial Magic on his own, without Dee's knowledge or consent. On May 7, 1584, the spirit Gabriel interrupted the dictation of the Keys to command Kelly to destroy certain items of his personal magical regalia:

> *Gabriel: All the trash thou hast of the wicked, burn it...*

> *E.K.: If Moses and Daniel were skilful in the Arts of the Egyptian Magicians, and were not therby hindered from being the servants of God, Why may not I deal with these, without hindrance to the Will of God?*

> *Gabriel: Darkness yieldeth unto light; the Great excludeth the lesser.*[12]

Kelly resisted these instructions, but finally conceded to the ritual destruction of a single talisman. Concerning the rest of this forbidden regalia, Kelly made the following remarks:

> *What I have done with the rest, God and they (if they be of God) know; upon the aforesaid conditions I am contented to have this Character be burnt.*[13]

It is curious to note that this ritual destruction was the first act of the May 14, 1584, working, on which the majority of the Angelic Keys was dictated. Thus we discover that Dee's ceremonial Magic was not the only occult influence upon Kelly. His own secretive magical practices must have had some effect upon his consciousness during the dictation of the Keys.

Kelly continued his illicit ceremonies, but he eventually became frightened at their results. On June 8, 1584, he confessed his practices to Dee, who was appalled at the revelation that his chosen "vessel" for communicating with Angels was indulging in what Dee called "horrendous, multiple heresies and blasphemous dogmas."

Kelly's involvement in heretical magical practices raises some questions which are vital to research into the origins of the Keys. What magical texts was Kelly using for his secret ceremonies, and what relation, if any, do these have to the Angelic Keys?

Israel Regardie states that "there is absolutely no trace of any part of the Angelic magical system of Angelic language in Europe,"[14] a viewpoint that was perhaps justified in its time. The Keys are, indeed, very different from the grimoires. The barbaric names in the *Lemegeton* are bastardized Arabic and Greek rather than a syntactically valid language like Enochian. However, there were grimoires attributed to

Enoch.[15] Could one of these been in Kelly's possession during the fateful period when the Keys were dictated?

If so, the grimoire must have been highly unusual and one with which Dee was unfamiliar. Where would Kelly locate such a treasure? As it happens, he had access to a source of unusual magical material. During the period of the Enochian dictations and Kelly's secret ceremonies, Dee and Kelly were living on St. Stephen's street in Cracow, within easy walking distance of the University of Cracow—the second oldest University in Eastern Europe, and a center for the study of the occult arts during the Renaissance.[16] It is reasonable to assume that Kelly would have been drawn to the university library in his consuming search for magical and alchemical knowledge.

Dee's diaries contain no mention of any visits to the university; so if Kelly went there, he probably went alone. We know that Kelly was doing surreptitious research, and that products of that research were appearing in his scrying, as shown in this passage from Dee's notes:

> "He [Kelly] came speedily out of his Study, and brought in his hand one volume of Cornelius Agrippa his works...whereupon he inferred, that our spiritual Instructors were Cosenors [frauds] to give us a description of the World, taken out of other Books...I replied and said, I am very glad that you have a Book of your own, wherin these Geographical names are expressed.[17]

It is possible, even likely, that the University of Cracow library contained manuscripts on Magic that originated in the heretical sects in Eastern Europe. Many of these sects were dedicated to Enoch, who was supposed to have been the original translator and communicator of the Angelic language. (Dee and Kelly believed that they were rediscovering something that had been lost.) One of these Enochian sects was responsible for the survival of a version of the *Book of Enoch*, a religious text so old that the only other extant version survived in distant and isolated Ethiopia.[18]

The notion that Kelly might have found the Angelic Keys in a heretical Enochian text remains entirely speculative unless some similarity, other than the vague attribution to Enoch, can be found between the Keys and the heretical Magical texts. The first indication of just such a connection is the philosophical viewpoint of the Keys, which has Gnostic overtones. For example, in the Call of the Thirty Aires, God states that he repents having made mankind. This is almost Manichaean in its rejection of the physical world and the human beings who live within it.

Beyond this, certain parallels to Enochian language can be found in early Gnostic texts, such as in the incantation known as the *Pistis Sophia*: "ZAMA ZAMA OZZA RACHAMA OZAI."[19] Note the repetition of the "Z" phoneme, a characteristic of Angelic, and the repetition of "ZAMA," which is very like the repeated "ZAMRAN" found in the Angelic Keys. "ZAMRAN" means "appear" in the Keys and is one the most important words in the conjurations. Another possible similarity can be found in the Gnostic name for the demiurge, "IALDABAOTH."[20] This is quite close to the Enochian God of Righteousness, "IAD BALTOH."

The *Pistis Sophia* also mentions books of Magic attributed to Enoch:

> *Ye shall find them in the two great Books of IEOU, which Enoch wrote when I spoke with him from the Tree of Knowledge, and from the Tree of Life, which were in the paradise of Adam.*[21]

The name IEOU suggest that the books contained conjurations or magical names, and the legendary origins of the texts in the garden of Eden is similar to the statement of Kelly's spirits that Angelic was the language "which Adam verily spoke in innocence." The Gnostic scholar Mead suggests that one of the books of IEOU is the *Book of the Great Logos*, a text that contains the following passage:

> *The guardians of the Gates of the treasure will open them, and they will pass upwards and ever inwards through the following spaces, and the powers rejoicing and giving them their mysteries, seals, and names of power; the Orders of the Three Amens... Within each treasure is a Door or Gate, and without three Gates; each of the outer gates has three guardians.*[22]

Compare the above passage with the following from Kelly's scrying during the period in which the Angelic Keys were dictated:

> *Every Table hath his key; every key openeth his gate, and every gate being opened, giveth knowledge of himself, or of his entrance, and of the mysteries of those things whereof he is an enclosure. Within these Palaces you shall find things that are of power, as well as to speak, for every (1) Palace is above his (2) City and every City is above his (3) Entrance.*[23]

Both the Gnostic Texts and the Angelic Keys place a great emphasis on the number forty-nine. For example, the *Pistis Sophia* states that, "the reflections of the supernal projections, powers, or co-partners of the Sophia [when] looked at from without, make an ordering into forty-nine."[24] The apocryphal *Books of the Savior* states that, "no mystery is higher than the mysteries ye seek after, save only the mystery of the Seven Voices and the Nine-and Forty Powers."[25]

The insistence upon the importance of the number forty-nine is echoed in the Enochian material from Edward Kelly:

> *[There are] 49 voices of calling; which are the Natural Keyes, to open...Gates of Understanding, wherby you shall have knowledge to move every Gate, and to call out as many as you please...and wisely open unto you the secrets of their Cities.*[26]

Contrast this passage with a similar passage in the *Book of the Great Logos*, where the forty-nine "powers" are connected to the "Gates of the Light-Treasure...and the Gates are opened unto them, and the Wardens give them their Seals and their Great Name."[27]

Kelly's secret ceremonies and researches in Cracow, the similarity of the Keys to certain Gnostic texts, as well as traces of Renaissance Angel Magic literature attributed to Enoch, all point to a textual rather than a spiritual origin for the Enochian Keys. Could the revelation of the Keys have been tied to a particular magical text located in the library at the University of Cracow? If so, then that manuscript may still be in the archives, waiting for some enterprising scholar to unearth it again.

❧

Was Kelly Actually in Communication with Angels?

A serious objection to the theory that Kelly plagiarized the keys is the way that they were revealed. The first five keys were dictated, letter by letter, backwards, while the rest were dictated forwards, without any significant errors. The bulk of the keys, over a thousand words, were dictated on a single day during a single session. Most of the English glosses were dictated on a single day, well after the Angelic, yet they match their Angelic counterparts almost perfectly. Kelly would have had to be capable of extraordinary feats of memory if he used another magical text as source material for the keys.

The notion that Kelly was actually communicating with Angels has been ignored by most scholars. Rather than reject the notion out of hand, perhaps it makes sense to critically analyze the communications themselves. Do they have any of the characteristics that we might expect from an actual communication with an Angelic presence? In fact, the Dee-Kelly ceremonies contain some evidence that suggests the presence of something unusual during some of the ceremonies.

One test for the presence of the supernatural is precognition of future events. This took place at least twice during the Dee-Kelly workings. The Angels predicted the Spanish Armada and the execution of Mary Queen of Scots well before those events could have been known.[28] On the other hand, the Angels predicted many other events that never took place, such as Lasky's role as a conquering hero.

A classic, though flawed, test for the validity of mediumistic and clairvoyant phenomena is the presence of a language which the scryer does not know. This occurred during the Dee-Kelly workings when one spirit began speaking in Greek. Kelly became frustrated and disturbed, and soon interrupted saying, "Unless you speak some language that I can understand, I will express no more of this Ghybbrish." This would seem proof of an exterior origin for Kelly's visions, especially because the Greek words warned Dee not to trust Kelly— an unlikely message for a charlatan to convey to his intended victim.

On the surface, there seems little reason for an Angel to need its own language at all. It is unlikely that an Angel, lacking vocal chords, would speak in a manner similar to human speech. This problem was pointed out by Leonardo Da Vinci: "Therefore we may say that the spirit cannot produce a voice without movement of the air and air in it there is none, nor can it emit what it has not."[29] In other words, a language uttered by Angels would have little or no relationship to any known grammatical system. It would have to be something like the Hebrew Cabala where concepts, numbers and energies are modulated to produce the unpronounceable name.

Thus any language that spirits would speak would be radically different from a language intended for use by human beings. Onomatopoeia—words like "bang" and "pop" which imitate actual sounds—would be totally lacking. Contractions would be used to create new concepts rather than to smooth pronunciation. Many words would feature strings of consonants rather than easily-pronounced mixtures of vowels and consonants. The letter arrangement would appear random and more like a Cabala than a spoken tongue; and finally, the system of numbers would not be based upon ten, because, along with a lack of vocal chords, non-material entities would have little use for fingers.

The Angelic language does, in fact, exhibit these characteristics. There are no onomatopoeias in Angelic. There are many contractions, such as *Telocvovim,* and many Angelic words feature unpronounceable strings of consonants. Angelic letter arrangements appear to be random, and the language is considered to be the source language for Hebrew, thus a Cabala is implied. Finally, Angelic numbers are incomprehensible using any known base or numbering scheme.

We can't rule out the possibility that Kelly was in touch with something outside of his own normal consciousness. It would appear that, for Dee and Kelly, Angel Magic actually worked, at least after a fashion. Kelly's Angels communicated more than just the Angelic language. Over time, the Angels increasingly took control of Dee's life and the lives of his family and followers. At the encouragement of the Angels, John Dee was about to enter the most unusual and dangerous period of his long and eventful life.

ZOPHIEL

The Result of Dee's Magic

hatever we think of the Angelic language and the Angelic Keys, Dee himself was extremely excited at this new revelation. Like most Angel Magi, Dee had a profound respect for Hebrew and the Cabala. This discovery of a language more ancient and more powerful than Hebrew seemed like the magical equivalent of atomic energy. Dee was desperate to follow up on this exciting turn in his research, even in the face of mounting pressures and problems.

THE HOLY ROMAN EMPEROR

Lasky was still not delivering on his promise of support and Dee's own money was beginning to run out. To make matters worse, Kelly had begun some private experiments and researches on his own. When Dee discovered that Kelly was moonlighting, he became extremely angry because he believed that Kelly's extracurricular activities would keep the true Angels from appearing. After a great deal of conflict and confusion, they finally completed the reception of the Angelic Keys, which the Angels told them would summon extremely powerful Angels who rule over different regions of the earth.

Dee felt that he was onto something. Growing tired of Lasky's lukewarm and unprofitable support, he decided, under strong encouragement from the Angels, to seek patronage at the court of Rudolph, Emperor of Germany. Furnished with letters of introduction by Lasky, Dee and Kelly traveled together to Prague, where they were later joined by their wives and servants.

Rudolph was a logical choice for Dee's next patron. He was interested in mystical and magical experiments and was known for supporting scholars, astrologers, and magicians. One of these was the astronomer John Kepler, who made Rudolph a magical drinking glass emblazoned with various planetary sigils.* Dee had every reason to think that he would be well received, possibly because Dee had once dedicated a book to Rudolph's father. In addition, the Angels were predicting that Rudolph, if he proved obedient to the Angel's suggestions, would become the greatest conqueror in the world, and even recapture Constantinople from the Turks.

Dee met with Rudolph only once. Rudolph seemed interested and Dee felt the interview had gone reasonably well; however, Rudolph did not permit Dee to visit him again. Instead, he sent a Doctor Curtzius to investigate Dee and Kelly. Dee "opened his books" to this Curtzius, who promised Dee a favorable report to the Emperor.

---

* Kepler later discovered the eliptical orbits of the planets, thereby proving Copernicus' theory that the planets moved around the sun rather than the earth. While there's no record of Dee and Kepler ever meeting, they were definitely kindred spirits. Dee had been a proponent of Copernicus since he was a young man.

Meanwhile, Edward Kelly was doing everything possible to undermine their position in the city. At one point Kelly became involved in a public brawl that did nothing to enhance the notion that Dee and Kelly were holy men who talked to Angels. This event is interesting because it reveals a great deal about Kelly's character and Dee's obvious exasperation at having to deal with such a volatile personality.

It happened one night[1] that Kelly was out drinking with a number of people including one Alexander, a servant of Lord Lasky's who had come with Dee and Kelly to Prague. Kelly became tipsy and, as part of some trivial quarrel, told Alexander that he "would cut off his head, and with his walking staff did touch him fair and softly on the neck."* Alexander, who was also drinking heavily, became angry and, "took those works in great snuff and went to defend himself and so took his weapon to him."

Alexander, drunk and maudlin, came over to Dee, and "wept much, complaining of E.K.'s words and the touch of the staff, and how it was against his credit to take that in good part and spake mostly soldier's terms of stout words that are not worthy of the recording....The watchmen perceiving Alexander's disquiet mind and hearing his words, came to me and charged me to have a care of the peace keeping. They further claimed that Alexander, in his rage, said that before E.K. could cut off his head, Alexander would cut him to pieces." Somehow Dee managed to quiet Alexander and placate the guards, who undoubtedly reported the incident to their superiors.

"The next morning E.K. came home and, seeing Alexander, apologized, pleading that he had been drunk." Dee, however, made the mistake of telling Kelly what Alexander had said in front of the watchmen. "No sooner had I expressed this then suddenly E.K. fell

---

* The quoted portions of the story are directly from Dee's diaries.

into such a rage, that he would be revenged of him for so saying and for railing on him in the street. Much ado had I to stop or hold him from going to Alexander with his weapon. At length we let him go in his doublet and hose, without a cap or hat on his head, and into the street he hastened with his brother's rapier drawn, and challenged Alexander to fight. But Alexander went from him, saying '*Nolo, Domine Kelleie, Nolo.*'* Hereupon E.K. took up a stone and threw it after him, as after a dog and so came into the house again, in most furious rage for that he might not fight with Alexander. The rage and fury was so great in words and gestures as might plainly prove that the wicked enemy sought to destroy either E.K. or me...."

FIGURE 21. SIR EDWARD KELLY[2]

---

* "I won't [fight], Lord Kelly, I won't [fight]."

Kelly's behavior made them look more like rogues than prophets. Perhaps as a consequence, Curtzius' reports to Rudolph were not complimentary. Dee was soon reduced to asking the Spanish ambassador to intercede with Rudolph on his behalf. This was a strange request because Spain was England's greatest enemy. Furthermore, Dee was known to have been involved in the planning of Drake's voyage around the world, a voyage that involved acts of war against Spanish colonies. That Dee would resort to asking the aid of an obvious enemy indicates his utter desperation at the current situation.

They were running low on money at this point with only the promises of the Angels to support them; and it was at this point that we get our only glimpse of Dee's long-suffering wife. She wrote a letter to the Angels, humbly requesting assistance to resolve their financial troubles. The letter seems both sad and sweet:

> We desire God of his great and infinite mercies, to grant us the help of these heavenly mysteries, that we may by them be directed how or by whom to be aided and relieved, in this necessity that we are in, of sufficient and needful provision, for meat and drink for us and our Family, wherewith we stand at this instant much opressed: and the rather because that might be hurtful to us, and the credit of the actions wherein we are vowed and linked unto his heavenly Majestie, (by the ministry and comfort of his holy Angels) to lay such things as are the ornaments of our House, and the coverings of our bodies, in pawn either unto such as a Rebels against his divine Majestie, the Jews, or the people of this City, which are malicious and full of wicked slanders: I Jane Dee humble request this thing of God, acknowledging myself his servant and handmaiden, to whom I commit my body and soul. (signed) Jane Dee.[3]

Evidently, it wasn't easy being the wife of an Angel Magus. The Angels replied by suggesting she keep inside the kitchen and not meddle with the things of God. Whatever else Kelly's Angels might have been, they certainly weren't politically correct.

Jane Dee's letter to the Angels helps us understand the attitude of Dee's entourage toward the Angels. The Angels—or rather Kelly's perception of the Angels—were calling the shots, telling the party where to go, who to contact, where to live, and what to do. Like the Shakers being led by Mother Ann's spirit guides or Mormons by Joseph Smith's golden tablets, Dee and company were operating on faith that the Angels knew what was best for all concerned.

In the spring of 1585, Dee received word from Lasky that Stephen, the King of Poland, was interested in Dee's experiments. Dee and Kelly hastily returned to Cracow, where they performed a number of ceremonies for this new potential patron.

Stephen became King of Poland by marriage, but soon proved his worth by fighting successfully against Ivan IV of Russia, and taking the city of Polotsk in 1582. He was a clever politician and a brave soldier—violent, cruel and intolerant. On official occasions, he was known to wear a gold helmet with round ear guards, a cloak made out of a flayed leopard, and a shield with an eagle's wing—feathers and all—nailed upon it. He used to have his horse painted bright red and shod with golden horseshoes. The horseshoes were attached loosely so that they would fall off during the procession, thereby illustrating that Stephen was so wealthy that gold was unimportant to him. (The shoes were, however, carefully gathered up afterwards by Stephen's servants.)

It seems somehow surprising that such a man would be interested in Dee's work; however, there was a strong interest in the occult in Stephen's family. Stephen was bred from the same stock that produced

Vlad Dracula, the crusader-cannibal upon which the fictional character of Count Dracula is based. Stephen's niece, Elizabeth Bathory, was
to be remembered as the cruelest woman in all of history. In an
alchemical experiment of her own, she bathed in the blood of hundreds of slain virgins, hoping that their life force would help her
remain young.

The Angels promised Stephen that Emperor Rudolph would be
assassinated and that Stephen would succeed him on the throne of
Germany. Stephen attended at least one ceremony, but did not think
the matter worth pursuing any further.

By this time, Dee was in desperate financial straits. Dee and Kelly
returned to Prague, but did not remain there long. A representative of
the Pope threatened to excommunicate Rudolph if he continued to
harbor English magicians and heretics at his court, and Dee and company were forced to flee. By a great stroke of luck they fell in with one
Count Rosenburg, a nobleman of considerable wealth, who let them
stay at his castle in Trebona in the kingdom of Bohemia.

THE TEST OF FAITH

It was in Rosenberg's castle in Trebona that Dee's faith in the Angels
was to face its greatest challenge. The Angels told Dee and Kelly that
they were to "hold their wives in common," a phrase that seemed to
mean that they should swap wives. Dee couldn't believe his ears. He
asked for a clarification, hoping that the suggestion was merely an
allegory for good Christian fellowship, but the Angels made it clear
that God expected Dee and Kelly to obey this instruction to the letter.

They did obey, and it is this incident more than any other, that was
responsible ruining Dee's reputation. To historians who believe in

Angels, such as Meric Casaubon who published Dee's diaries in 1654, the wife-swapping is proof that Dee was being deceived by devils. To historians who don't believe in Angels, Dee was merely being deceived by Kelly, who lusted after Dee's wife. Dee's participation in what seems like a patently obvious scheme made him look like such fool that it seemed to negate all of his previous accomplishments.

Both opinions are unrealistic. The truth was at once more simple and more complex than this. Dee and Kelly had, under the Angels' tutelage, created their own cult where Kelly's Angels were making the decisions. It is not unusual for religious cults to symbolize their uniqueness through the adoption of unorthodox sexual practices. The Shakers, for example, enforced total celibacy. The early Mormons adopted polygamy. In more recent times, the Branch Davidians of the Seventh Day Adventists married all their females to a single man. When seen in this light, the wife-swapping scheme merely becomes a logical extension of the situation in which Dee and Kelly found themselves.

This is not to say that there weren't significant psychological pressures within Dee's entourage. It is entirely likely that there was a degree of sexual energy between the two friends and their wives.

Both Dee and Kelly clearly thought the act of wife swapping was a test of faith. Dee, for example, was horrified at the very idea, and began to call the Angels "apparitions," as if questioning their very reality. The two wives "disliked utterly this last doctrine," and wanted no part of it. Kelly's reaction to the request was to become extremely angry and insist that the swapping request proved that the Angels were devils. It has been suggested that Kelly was cleverly hiding his inner feelings of lust with an outward show of mock indignation. This interpretation, however, is over-subtle. It is unlikely that a liar and seducer would have been so vociferous in his objections, lest they prove too convincing to his intended victims.

I think the wife-swapping was exactly as the Angels claimed it to be—a test. Dee and company were no longer Christians. Through this unique act, they became a tightly-knit community that shared a secret bond, an act that, if made known, would result in condemnation from the outside world. As Kelly's Angels put it:

> Behold these four, who is he that shall say they have sinned? Unto whom shall they make account? Not unto you, you sones of men, nor unto your children, for unto the Lord belongeth the judgement of his servants.[4]

SUCCESS AT LAST

Whatever one thinks of the wife-swapping incident, there's little doubt that Dee and Kelly's Angel Magic became very strange immediately after they performed the act.

First, the nature of their communications with Angels changed. In earlier ceremonies, the Angels seemed extraordinarily pious. Now the Angels began dictating passages that were filled with sexual imagery:

> I am the daughter of fortitude and am ravished every hour. My feet are swifter than the winds and my hands are sweeter than the morning dew. I am deflowered and yet a virgin. In the night season I am sweet and in the day full of pleasure. I am a harlot for such as ravish me and a virgin with such as know me not. For lo, I am loved of many and I am a lover to many. Cast out your old strumpets and burn their clothes; abstain from the company of other women that are defiled, that are sluttish, and not so handsome and beautiful as I. And then I will come and dwell amongst you

and, behold, I will bring forth children unto you. I will
open my garments and stand naked before you that your
love may be more enflamed.[5]

This "sexualizing" of the Angelic visions matched the sexualizing of
the relations between Dee, Kelly, and their wives.

Another, much more important change also took place at this time.
Up until this point, Dee remained a passive observer. All his contact
with the Angels had been through Kelly's eyes and ears. Dee had seen
nothing for himself. Now, however, things began to happen that Dee
could see with his own eyes:

There appeared a great flame of fire in the principal Stone
(both standing on the table before E.K.)...Suddenly one
seemed to come in at the forth window of the Chappel...the
stone was heaved up a handful high and set down again.
The one at the window seemed...with spread-abroad arms
to come to E.K., at which sight, he shrinked back somewhat,
and then that Creature took up between both his hands the
stone and frame of gold, and mounted up away as he came.
E.K. catched at it, but he could not touch it...E.K. was in a
great fear and trembling and had tremorem cordis* for a
while. But I was very glad and well pleased.[6]

Dee was "glad and well-pleased" because he at last had the physical
evidence that he needed to convince himself that the experiments
were truly valid. Up until this point, he had depended upon faith and
a certain unaccountable trust of Kelly's basic character. Now he had
the evidence of his own eyes to prove that he was on the right track.

If you don't accept the notion that Dee and Kelly were communicating with Angels, then there are only three ways to explain this

---

* Heart tremors.

event: One, Dee made it up and wrote it down in his diary; two, Dee was hallucinating; or, three, Kelly was working some kind of stage illusion. None of the three explanations is quite satisfactory.

The first explanation doesn't make sense because Dee's diaries were clearly for his own use. Why would Dee write lies in a document that was meant for his eyes only? The second explanation—that Dee was hallucinating—isn't logical either. Why would Dee suddenly begin hallucinating? If he were to hallucinate, one would think that he would start seeing the same Angels that Kelly was describing in such detail. The third explanation—that Kelly was working a stage illusion—at first seems like the only explanation; but there are serious objections here as well. The most obvious is that Dee was already famous for his ability to work stage illusions. (Remember the "magical" flying scarab?) Kelly was about as likely to fool Dee as you or I would be to fool an accomplished stage magician by using a child's card trick.

Another objection is that the stage magic of the Renaissance simply wasn't well enough developed to accomplish the illusion in question. Making a heavy crystal sphere fly through the air and out a window, and then retrieving it unharmed, would be a mystifying trick even today. It would have been impossible during a time when the following trick, from a book published in 1584, was considered a state-of-the-art routine.

> Take a verie great ball in your left hand, or three indifferent big balles; and shewing one or three little balles, seeme to put them into your said left hand, concealing (as you may well doo) the other balles which were there before: then use words, and make them seeme to swell, and open your hand. &c.[7]

The third and final objection to the stage illusion theory is that the timing is wrong. Why would Kelly wait until after the wife-swapping incident to prove the reality of the Angelic communications? If he had had designs on Dee's wife, wouldn't it have made more sense to provide this dramatic demonstration beforehand, when Dee was questioning the entire affair?

None of the three explanations for the levitation event are entirely satisfactory. We are forced to at least consider the fact that Dee and Kelly experienced something that lies outside of the current understanding of science. If so, it would seem that Dee was correct when he believed they had tapped into something quite powerful.

Another interesting indication that something unusual was going on was that Dee believed he had succeeded in transmuting base metal into gold. According to at least one source, a December night in 1586, Dee cut a piece of metal out of a brass warming pan, heated it, and added the elixir, converting it into pure silver. He then sent the warming pan and the piece of silver to Queen Elizabeth so she could see that he had succeeded in his alchemical experiments. At the same time, Dee and Kelly started spending money as if they had enough to burn. Kelly is rumored to have given away four thousand pounds sterling worth of gold rings during the marriage celebration of one of his maidservants.[8]

The Queen's Magus

Did Dee and Kelly succeed in finding the philosopher's stone and transmuting base metals into silver and gold? Dee's contemporaries certainly believed they had. Their apparent success did not, however, keep Dee and Kelly from parting a short time afterwards.

The Firstborn Slain

Kelly left Dee and entered the service of Emperor Rudolph. Since Rudolph had been unswervingly hostile to Dee and Kelly, the only explanation for this was that the Emperor also believed that Dee and Kelly had succeeded where so many had failed. While Kelly was in the Emperor's service, he wrote a book on alchemy which makes no direct mention of either Dee or Angel Magic; but does contain an oblique reference to Dee, which leads one to believe that they parted friends. Kelly writes in his preface addressed to Rudolph:

> *A familiar acquaintance with different branches of knowl-edge has taught me this one thing, that nothing is more ancient, excellent, or more desirable than truth, and who-ever neglects it must pass his whole life in the shade. Nevertheless, it always was, and always will be, the way of mankind to release Barabbas and to crucify Christ.*[9]

Kelly had good reason to complain. The Emperor had changed Kelly's status from that of an honored guest to that of a prisoner. Kelly, it seems, was unable to reproduce the success he and Dee had enjoyed at Trebona, even though Dee had left him the elixir and alchemical implements they had used. The emperor quite naturally assumed that Kelly was keeping the secrets of transmutation from him. Imprisoned in a tower, Kelly died in 1595, while trying to escape down a ladder made of sheets.[10] According to the story, he had grown too fat for the improvised rope to hold his weight.

By this time Dee was already in England. In 1589, Dee traveled back to England in the grandest style, more like an ambassador than a private citizen. He had three coaches, with four horses for each course, a number of loaded wagons, and guard of up to twenty-four soldiers to protect him on the journey. The Queen traveled to Rich-mond to greet him personally.

Elizabeth probably believed, as did the rest of the world at the time, that Dee had found the philosopher's stone. It is likely that she was very interested in the Angel Magic which Dee believed was the source of his success. Elizabeth gave special orders that Dee should remain free to attempt whatever experiments he wished, either alchemical or Magical. This was the opportunity that Dee had been waiting for. He now had the backing of a major monarch and the funds to pursue his research.

Dee's Magical diaries from this period have been completely lost. Because much of the rest of Dee's Magical records have survived, it is possible that the diaries from this period were intentionally destroyed. If so, this may be because Elizabeth and key members of her court were directly involved in Dee's Angel Magic. The population at large was highly skeptical of Angel Magic, and it would have been very dangerous politically for the Queen's involvement to be known.

Whether or not Dee's Angel Magic in this period was successful is open to question. What is definite is that his experiments were well financed. The British museum still contains a solid gold talisman based upon Dee's Angel Magic. Such an expensive item would not have been possible without the patronage of somebody with extreme wealth.

The probable liaison between Dee and Elizabeth was none other than Sir Walter Raleigh. He was involved in the practice of alchemy and the occult,[11] and Dee was associated with Raleigh at this time, forming an alternative university for the study of subjects not covered at Oxford or Cambridge.[12] They were joined by a number of interesting characters including Henry Percy (the so-called "wizard earl"), the poet John Donne, and the playwright Christopher Marlowe.

Betrayal and Disgrace

It was Christopher Marlowe who put an end to Dee's royal support and sanction. He produced a play that sharply satirized Dee, a play that made it impossible for Elizabeth to continue to support Dee's experiments, either publicly or privately.

The play was *Doctor Faustus*, probably one of the most controversial works of the Elizabethan era. We'll probably never know why Marlowe betrayed his erstwhile friends, but it is a historical fact that the play was an immediate sensation. The special effects, which included make-believe devils with fireworks spouting out of their mouths, were equaled by the realism of the Angel Magic practiced on the stage. It was so realistic and so impressive that a hundred years later it was still believed that a real demon had materialized during one of the early presentations of the play.[13]

The audiences who watched *Doctor Faustus* were terrified by the play, which encouraged a growing intolerance toward Angel Magic that was increasingly directed at Dee and his group of occult experimenters. Although the play was ostensibly based upon a semi-historical wizard named John Faust, contemporary audiences immediately recognized that Marlowe's character was a parody of the famous John Dee.

The parallels between Faustus and Dee are clear from the moment that Faustus speaks. The following gives a comparison of the text of the play with entries from Dee's own diaries. From *Doctor Faustus*:

> *Settle thy studies, Faustus, and begin to sound the depth of that thou wilt profess. Is to dispute well logic's chiefest end? Affords this art no greater miracle? Then read no more; thou hast attained that end. A greater subject fitteth Faustus' wit. Be a physician, Faustus, heap up gold and be eternalized for*

*some wondrous cure. What, Faustus, hast thou not attained
that end? Are not thy bills hung up as monuments whereby
whole cities have escaped the plague? Physic, farewell. What
of the law? A petty case of paltry legacies! This study fits a
mercenary drudge who aims at nothing but external trash.
These necromantic books are heavenly. Oh, what a world of
profit and delight, of power, of honour, of omnipotence, is
promised to the studious artizan. All things that move
between the quiet poles shall be at my command. Tis magic,
magic that hath ravished me.*[14]

From Dee's Diary:

*I have from my youth up, desired and prayed unto God for
pure and sound wisdom and understanding of truths natural and artificial, so that God's wisdom, goodness, and
power bestowed in the frame of the world might be brought
in some bountiful measure under the talent of my capacity...
So for many years and in many places, far and near, I have
sought and studied many books in sundry languages, and
have conferred with sundry men, and have laboured with
my own reasonable discourse, to find some inkling, gleam,
or beam of those radical truths. But after all my endeavors I
could find no other way to attain such wisdom but by the
Extraordinary Gift, and not by any vulgar school, doctrine,
or human invention."... Therefore I was sufficiently taught
and confirmed that I would never attain this wisdom by
man's hand or by human power, but only from God, directly
or indirectly.*[15]

Marlowe clearly had Dee in mind when he had Doctor Faustus make
visits to the Holy Roman Emperor and to the Pope. These were dis-
torted versions of Dee's travels on the continent. Marlowe's Faustus

reaffirmed in the popular imagination that Angel Magic was not only real but damnable. This was bad news for John Dee. According to the noted scholar Frances Yates, Marlowe's propaganda played a considerable part in the decline of Dee's reputation and in the ability of Elizabeth and her court to give him patronage. This was because Marlowe's *Doctor Faustus* associated Dee, and by extension the entire notion of the Renaissance magus, with the worship of devils. This was hardly the sort of thing likely to endear the ruling class to the populace.[16]

Perhaps as a result of his indiscretion, Marlowe was soon killed under highly mysterious circumstances. According to testimony at the time, Marlowe was in danger of bringing "some great men" into a public scandal, and there were those in high places who were interested in seeing that "the mouth of so dangerous a member might be stopped."

Marlowe was silenced, but the damage was already done. The Queen and court could no longer support Dee either openly or clandestinely. Lacking royal patronage, Dee's Angel Magic collapsed and he was forced to retire, taking on the wardenship of the college at Manchester, a position he held until a few years before his death.

THE FINAL EXILE

As he grew older, Dee began to complain of poverty and various difficulties. The money he was to have received from his church positions never materialized. Furthermore, his library and laboratory had been looted and burned while he was away in Europe. He expected Elizabeth to reimburse him for these losses, but while Elizabeth did send him two or three small sums of money, no major sums were forthcoming.

Dee's letters from the period seem querulous and bitter. He was growing old—as was his patron—and he probably missed the glory of his former circumstances. At length he receded altogether from public life and retired to his ancient domicile at Mortlack. He became increasingly obsessed with clearing his name of the charge of having practiced black Magic. He even asked King James, after Elizabeth's death, to put him on trial for witchcraft. Luckily for Dee, James ignored the aging wizard's request.

Dee practiced Angel Magic to the end of his days. As late as a year before his death, his diaries record that he was trying to use Angel Magic to discover treasure buried in the earth. He was not successful and, in fact, was forced to sell his precious books just to keep himself fed. He died in 1608, neglected and forgotten, although not entirely.

There was another play about a magician, a play that returned to the vision of the Angel Magus as a powerful force that ultimately worked for the good of mankind. It was Shakespeare's *The Tempest*, the magician was Prospero, and these words—the last that Shakespeare ever wrote—are a fitting epitaph to the life of Doctor John Dee:

Now my charms are all o'verthrown,
And what strength I have's my own,
Which is most faint...now I lack
Spirits to enforce, art to enchant,
And my ending is despair,
Unless I be relieve'd by prayer,
Which pierces so that it assaults
Mercy itself and frees all faults.
As you from crimes would pardon'd be
Let your indulgence set me free.[17]

RAPHAEL DESCENDING TO EARTH

7

Fairy Magic

As interest in Angel Magic grew, it became part of the popular culture of the Renaissance. As a result, a new form of Magic—Fairy Magic—developed as a method to control the nature spirits that were part of the folklore of the people.

According to popular opinion, Angel Magic was very dangerous. Although an Angel Magus might have the highest ideals and intend only to communicate with good Angels, there was always the danger of deceit. Indeed, John Dee was popularly believed to have been deceived by evil spirits even when he thought he was communicating with God's most holy creatures.

The populace at large wanted a safe form of Angel Magic and Fairy Magic fulfilled that need. The Fairy folk were believed by many to have been neutral angels that did not participate in the conflict between good and evil. Fairy folk inhabited the woods and meadows, and were familiar and homely, and not likely to lead a would-be Angel Magus into sin or self-destruction.

EARLY FAIRY MAGIC

Some of the earliest recorded rituals of Fairy Magic appear in a seven-teenth century manuscript, although the style of the Latin indicates an earlier period. The rituals we will examine begin with an incanta-tion to summon the fairy queen (literally: queen of the pigmies), a legendary entity who can be linked to the mother goddess of ancient Britain. The incantation is Christian in character, and the theory implied is that the name of God has power over the queen. I give the incantation in the original Latin doggerel:

> *Micol o tu micoll regina pigmeorum deus Abraham: deus Isacc: deus Jacob: tibi benedicat et omnia fausta danet it concedat. Modo venias et mihi moremgem veni. Igitur o tu micol in nomine Jesus veni cito ters quatur beati in qui nomini Jesu veniunt veni. Igitur O tu micol in nomine Jesu veni cito qui sit omnis honor laus et gloria in omne aeter-num. Amen Amen.*[1]

The next ritual, from a different manuscript, is an attempt to dis-miss the guardian spirits from a secret treasure hoard. The guardian spirits have names that suggest Latin origin, another indication of the antiquity of the belief in such spirits. It is possible that the ritual may be related to earlier rituals current in Britain at a time when the Roman ruins had not been completely plundered.*

---

* I have tried to preserve the flavor of the original text, altering it only as required to clarify the meaning for a modern reader.

FIGURE 22. WITCHES CONJURING FAIRIES[2]

A discharge of the fayres and other spirits or Elphes from any place or grounde, where treasure is layd or hidd. First shall the magician say "in the name of the father, the sonne, & the holy Ghost, amen" and then say as followeth: "I conjure you spirits or elphes which be 7 sisters and have these names: Lilia, Restilia, Foca, Fola, Afryca, Julia, Venuilia. I conjure youe & charge you by the father, the sonne, & the holy Ghost and holy Mary the mother of our blessed lord and Savior Jesus Christ and by the annunicateion, nativity and circumcision, and by the baptisme, and by his holy fasting, and by the passion, death and reserection of our blessed lord Jesus Christ and by the Comeing of the holy gost our sacred Comforter, and by all the Apostles, Martyres, and confessors, and also virgins and all the elect of God and of our lord Jesus Christ, that from hensforth neither you nor any other of you have power or rule upon this ground, neither within nor without nor uppon this servant of the liveing god, (name), neither by day nor night, but by the holy trinity be always upon itt & him or her. Amen. Amen."[3]

The next ritual illustrates a long-standing tradition in Angel Magic—the imprisonment of the spirit in a crystal glass or mirror. This method of Angel Magic is related in the *Lemegeton*, which contains a brief explanation of the magical bottle in which Solomon imprisoned demons. The curious combination of folk herbology and high Magic, combined with the absence of Christian elements, except for the use of holy water links the following ritual closely to remnants of Pagan practices in Renaissance Britain.

An excellent way to gett a Faryrie...that is not allready bound. First gett a broad square christall or Venus glasse in length and breadth 3 inches. Then lay that glasse or christall in the bloud of a white henne 3 wednesdayes or 3 fridayes. Then take it out and wash it with holy water and fumigate it. Then take 3 hazle stickes or wands of a year's groth, peel them fayre and white, and make soe longe as you write the spiritts name or fayries name, which you call 3 times, on every sticke being made flatt one side, then bury them under some hill whereas you suppose fayries haunt, the Wednesday before you call her, and the Friday followinge take them uppe and call hir at 8 or 3 or 10 of the clocke which be good plannetts and howres for that turne. But when you call, be in cleane Life and turne thy face towards the east, and when you have her bind her to that stone or Glasse.[4]

A recipe for a magical ointment is also included in the ceremony:

An unguent to annoynt under the Eyelids* and upon the Eylidds evninge and morninge, but especially when you call, or finde your sight not perfect. (That is, an ointment to give sight of the fairies.) Put salad oyle and put it into a Viall glasse but first wash it with rose water, and marygold flower water, the flowers be gathered towards the east. Wash it til the oyle come white, then put it into the glasse, and thou put thereto the budds of holyhocke, the flowers of mary gold, the flowers or toppes of wild thyme, the budds of younge hazle, and the thyme must be gatherred neare the side of a hill where the fayries use to go oft, and the grasse of a fayrie throne, there, all these putt into the oyle, into the glasse, and set it to dissolve 3 days in the sonne, and thou keep it for thy use.[5]

---

* Needless to say, one should always use the greatest caution bringing any foreign substance close to the eyes. Neither the author nor the publisher recommends the use of this ointment and any attempt to use the recipe is completely at the practitioner's own risk.

CHARITY, HOPE AND FAITH

The next ritual is taken from a highly Christianized ceremony to conjure a fairy named "Elaby Gathen." The magical names included in the incantation form a link to Gnostic Angel Magic texts. It is a straightforward conjuration, again attempting to bind a fairy into a magical glass.

> *I [name] call thee Elaby Gathen in the name of the father, of the sonne and of the holy ghost and I adjure thee, Elaby Gathen, conjure and straightly charge and command thee by Tetragrammaton, Emanuell, Messias, Sether, Panton, Cratons, Alpha et Omega, and by all other high and reverent names of all-mightly god, both effable and ineffable and by all the vertues of the holy ghost by the dyetic grace and foreknowledge of the powers and grace and vertues of thee, Elaby, by all the powers and grace and vertues of all the holy meritorious Virginnes and patriarches. And I conjure thee, Elaby Gathen, by these holy names of God: Sday, Eloy, Iskyros, Adonay, Sabaoth, that thou appeare presently, meekely and myldly in this glasse without doeing hurt or daunger unto me or any other livinge creature and to this I bind thee by the whole power and vertue of our Lord Jesus Christ.*[6]

THE CONJURATION OF SIBYLIA

A far more elaborate example of Fairy Magic was published by Reginald Scot in 1584. I have excerpted portions of the ceremony, removing repetitious citations to the Christian hierarchy. This ritual is an excellent example of a fairy conjuration, combining elements of Christianity, Judaism, and Paganism.

I conjure thee Sibylia, O gentle virgine of fairies, and by all the angels of Jupiter and their characters and vertues, and by all the spirits of Jupiter and Venus and their characters and vertues, and by all the characters that be in the firmament, and by the king and queene of fairies, and their vertues, and by the faith and obedience that thou bearest unto them. I conjure thee Sibylia by the bloud that ranne out of the side of our Lord Jesus Christ crucified, and by the opening of heaven, and by the renting of the temple, and by the darkenes of the sunne in the time of his death, and by the rising up of the dead in the time of his resurrection, and by the virgine Marie mother of our Lord Jesus Christ, and by the unspeakable name of God, Tetragrammaton. I conjure thee, O Sibylia, O blessed and beautifull virgine, by all the riall words aforesaid; I conjure thee Sibylia by all their vertues to appeare in that circle before me visible, in the forme and shape of a beautifull woman in a bright and vesture white, adonred and garnished most faire, and to appeare to me quickly without deceipt or tarrieng, and that thou faile not to fulfill my will and desire...[7]

The successful binding of a faery was believed to procure many benefits. For example, the following ritual calls Sibylia for the purpose of obtaining a ring of invisibility.

I conjure you three sisters of fairies, Milia, Achilia, Sibylia, by the father, by the sonne, and by the Holie-ghost and by their vertues and powers, and by the most mercifull and living God, that will command his angell to blowe the trumpe at the daie of judgement; and he shall saie, Come, come, come to judgement; and by all angels, archangels, thrones, dominations, pricipats, potestates, virtues, cherubim and seraphim, and by their vertues and powers. I conjure you

*three sisters, by the vertue of all the riall words aforesaid: I
charge you that you doo appeare before me visiblie, in forme
and shape of faire women, in white vestures, and to bring
with you to me, the ring of invisibilitie, by the which I may
go invisible at mine owne will and pleasure, and that in all
houres and minutes. In nomine patriss, & filii, & spiritus
sancti, Amen.*[8]

This type of Angel Magic was practiced during the Renaissance, as
we can see from a trial in 1576 described by Sir Walter Scott:.

*He showed her a company of eight women and four men.
The women were busked in their plaid and very seemly. The
strangers saluted her, and said, "Welcome, Bessie; wilt thou
go with us?" But Bessie was silent...After this she saw their
lips move, but did not understand what they said and in a
short time they removed from thence with a hideous ugly
howling sound, like that of a hurricane. [The conjurer]
then acquainted her that these were the good wights (fairies
dwelling in the court of Elfland, who came to invite her to
go thither with them. Bessie answered, that before she went
that road, it would require some consideration....*[9]

THE FAIRY SEERS

Fairy Magic remained in the folklore of the countryside. A new type of
Angel Magus emerged, the "tabhaisver," who could perceive and sometimes control the local hobgoblins. This was not always a welcome gift.
The tabhaisver described in the following passage was evidently afraid
of his power.

> *The TABHAISVER, or Seer, that corresponds with this*
> *kind of Familiars, can bring them with a Spel to appear to*
> *himselfe or others when he pleases, as readily as Endor*
> *Witch to those of her Kind. He tells, they are ever readiest to*
> *go on hurtfull Errands, but seldome will be the Messengers*
> *of great Good to Men. He is not terrified with their Sight*
> *when he calls them, but seeing them in a surprize (as often*
> *he does) frights him extreamly. And glad would he be quit*
> *of such, for the hideous Spectacles seen among them, as the*
> *torturing of some Wight, earnest ghostly staring Looks, Skir-*
> *mishes , and the like.*[10]

The method of conjuration used by the tabhaisver was less complex than the rituals of the high Renaissance. Note that the beautiful virgins of the earlier conjurations have been replaced by some type of troll or goblin.

> *The usewall Method for a curious Person to get a transient*
> *Sight of this otherwise invisible Crew of Subterraneans, (if*
> *impotently and over rashly sought) is to put his left Foot*
> *under the Wizard's right Foot, and the Seer's Hand is put*
> *on the Inquirer's Head, who is to look over the Wizard's*
> *right Shoulder...then will he see a Multitude of Wight's like*
> *furious hardie Men, flocking to him haistily form all Quar-*
> *ters, as thick as Atoms in the Air, which are no Nonentities*
> *or Phantasms, Creatures proceiding from an affrighted*
> *Apprehensione, confused or crazed Sense, but Realities,*
> *appearing to a stable Man in his awaking Sense, and*
> *enduring a rationall Tryall of their Being.*[11]

The tabhaisvers inherited the tradition of Fairy Magic and were in part responsible for the incorporation of Angel Magic rituals into the folk religion of rural Britain. Even as late as the reign of Queen Victoria, gifted individuals called "taishers" were believed to have the power to perceive strange beings. This gift was said to be controllable with prayer.

> *A taisher in Caolas, Tiree, was observed to have great objections to going home to take his meals. Being questioned on the subject, he said that at home he saw a horrible-looking black woman, with her head "as black as a pot," and if he chanced to catch a glimpse of her at meal-times, her hideous appearance made him rise from his food...It was a belief in the island of Coll that a person afflicted with the second Sight might get rid of his unhappy gift, and, as it were, bind it away from himself, by giving alms and praying the gift may depart.*[12]

Fairy Magic has the distinction of being the only form of Angel Magic to be practiced unchanged from the Renaissance almost into the current century. While it has since died out in that form, the conjuration of Fairies and nature spirits may be destined for a future revival.

BEHOLD NOW BEHEMOTH

Angel Magic
and the Golden Dawn

ngel Magic had degenerated into fairy and folk lore, and as a result, ceased to be of interest to most educated men. The so-called Age of Reason was approaching. The decline of interest in Angel Magic was the direct result of the collapse of the philosophical underpinnings upon which the Magic was based. Most educated people either didn't believe in Angels or didn't believe that they intervened in the affairs of men. Even those priests and theologians who believed in direct angelic intervention rejected the notion that the conjurations of the magician were capable of controlling such exalted creatures.

～

AFTER THE RENAISSANCE

Angel Magic moved out of the philosophical mainstream, becoming of more interest to the historian and antiquarian than the practicing magician. One such antiquarian, Elias Ashmole, was responsible for the survival of many of the magical manuscripts that might otherwise have been lost. In particular, he gathered and preserved the manuscripts and

remaining library of Doctor Dee. In later years, Ashmole even attempted
to reproduce Dee's Angel Magic experiments. Ashmole is a particularly
interesting figure because, in addition to being a practicing Angel
Magus, he was an early Freemason. The origin of Freemasonry remains a
mystery, but it is clear from Ashmole's early involvement in the movement—as well as numerous later developments—that the Freemasonry
originally had a strong occult flavor to it.

Other than Ashmole's attempt to revive Dee's Angel Magic, the
energies of the mystical and religious thinkers after the Renaissance
were focused in other directions. In 1659, Meric Casaubon published
excerpts from Dee's magical diaries. Casaubon's edition publicized the
fact that Dee and Kelly had been wife-swapping, an event not likely to
endear Angel Magic to the public at large. This not only destroyed
what was left of Dee's reputation, it made philosophers of the period
think of Angel Magic as something disreputable, more of a con game
than an exalted search for "radical knowledge." This attitude was popularized by the playwright Ben Jonson in *The Alchemist*, where a
Dee-like figure swindles a number of foolish citizens.

Mystics were still interested in Angels, of course. Mystics of the seventeenth century, like Jacob Boehme and Robert Fludd, kept many of
the ideas of Angel Magic alive, without suggesting that people actually
practice Angel Magic ceremonies. In the late seventeenth century,
there was a brief revival of interest in Angel Magic in the writings of
the Swedish scientist and mystic Emanuel Swedenborg. Swedenborg
was originally a research theorist on geology and mining. In 1745 he
turned to the study of mysticism. While it is unlikely that Swedenborg performed any ceremonies resembling those in the medieval
grimoires, he did use controlled breathing to produce a trance-like
state, in which he would see visions of God and the Angels, which he
then recorded in a voluminous collection of works.

Boehme, Fludd and Swedenborg all had an influence on the visionary English poet and artist William Blake. Blake stated many times in his writings that his poems and paintings were inspired by visions. Blake created a number of long and complicated engravings, full of powerful illustrations that form a huge cosmic drama of conflict between otherworldly beings. It is very possible that Blake was familiar with the Hebraic tradition of Angel Magic. One of his so-called "minor prophesies" is *Tiriel* (1789), the title of which suggests a familiarity with Hebraic Angelic names.

Even this watered-down Angel Magic represented a philosophical backwater. Angel Magic did not fit well into the world view of the Enlightenment. The men of the eighteenth century were far more interested in trade, technology and government than they were in talking to Angels. Angel Magic was based upon the concept that knowledge could be extracted directly from the mind of God. Now that philosophical underpinning was withdrawn, as thinkers of the period looked to the scientific method to reveal the secrets of nature and the universe. Trial and Error replaced Angels and Demons as the way to advance the fortunes and future of mankind.

While Angel Magic fell into disrepute, books and manuscripts containing rituals continued to surface from time to time. In 1801, for example, large portions of Agrippa's *De Occulta Philosophia* were republished in *The Magus*, edited by Francis Barrett; but interest in Angel Magic had subsided to such a degree that the publication went virtually unnoticed. Other than the Fairy Magic still being practiced by ignorant peasants in the countryside, it looked like Angel Magic was about to die out completely.

ARCHANGEL MICHAEL SLAYING A DRAGON

THE GOLDEN DAWN

Then, in the late nineteenth century, a renewal of Angel Magic began with a group of Freemasons. The two principle movers in this revival were S.L. Macgregor Mathers and Dr. Wynn Westcott, who founded The Hermetic Order of the Golden Dawn. Other important members of the Order included the magical scholar A.E. Waite, the poet W.B. Yeats, and the bad boy of Angel Magic, Aleister Crowley.

The founding of the Golden Dawn is a matter of some controversy. In 1972, Ellic Howe published a documentary history of the Golden Dawn entitled *The Magicians of the Golden Dawn.*[1] In the first chapter, he accuses the founders, Westcott and Mathers, of fabricating the documents that led to the founding. Howe's assessment of the evidence is full of logical inconsistencies; and, far from settling the question, he succeeds only in making an already muddy situation even more confusing.

Howe's analysis is based upon a set of documents that provided the "charter" for the order,* and consisted of a manuscript outlining some rituals, in a simple substitution code, and generally referred to as "the cipher manuscript; and a set of letters from Germany, most of which were apparently authored by one Fraulein Sprengel, purported to be a representative of the "Secret Chiefs," a group of somewhat mysterious illuminatii.

Mathers and Westcott believed the cipher manuscript was old, if not ancient. Howe disagrees, quoting A.E. Waite's opinion that the cipher manuscript dates from as late as 1870. He attempts to buttress

---

* Howe refuses to give the location and ownership of the originals of these documents on the grounds that the owner doesn't wish to be pestered by inquiries.

Waite's dating by pointing out that a name, "Pereclinis Faustis," that appears in the 1877 edition of Mackenzie's *Royal Masonic Encyclopedia* also appears in the cipher manuscript. Because Howe wasn't able to find the name in any other earlier English work, he concludes that the name in the cipher must have been copied out of Mackenzie.

The problem with relying upon Waite for dating magical manuscripts is that he consistently underestimates the antiquity of magical texts. In his *Book of Ceremonial Magic*, for example, Waite estimates the age of medieval grimoires based upon relatively modern additions to the text, ignoring the elements that are clearly of great antiquity. Howe's argument in support of Waite's dating is feeble at best. The name, Pereclinis Faustis, could just as easily been copied from the cipher manuscript into Mackenzie, or both works could have both gotten the name from some other source. The fact that Howe couldn't find an earlier reference is irrelevant. Anyone who's worked with magical manuscripts quickly learns that there are almost always sources of material hidden away in lost or forgotten manuscripts. The fact that Howe could not find an earlier reference doesn't mean that one doesn't exist.

Having thus "dated" the manuscript, Howe proceeds to ignore the only hard evidence concerning the manuscript's actual date—the fact that the pages of the original cipher manuscript have a 1809 watermark and are written in faded ink. Because Howe has already decided that the manuscript was written in the 1870s, he assumes that the document was intentionally doctored to appear old. Howe would have us believe that Westcott and Mathers located some old paper and used artificially faded ink merely to impress the people that they wanted to recruit into the lodge.

Unfortunately, this doesn't make sense. If Westcott and Mathers wanted to impress, wouldn't they have found paper that was much older than 1809? Why would they go to all that bother just to push the date of the manuscript back sixty years? It is far more likely that the cipher manuscript in its current form dates from around 1809, although it might be a copy of an older document. Howe's dating of the manuscript, and belief that it was artificially aged, simply can't be taken seriously.

Howe then proceeds to criticize Westcott's story that Eliphas Levi—a famous French Magus of the preceding generation—once possessed the original of the cipher manuscript. Howe states that Levi "knew little English and if he ever had the cipher manuscript it would not have meant much to him." Here again Howe isn't thinking logically. Even if Levi weren't fluent in English, he would easily have recognized that the document was English and could have gotten someone to translate it for him.

Similarly, Howe tries to debunk Westcott's statements that the Cipher manuscript was "Rosicrucian,"* pointing out that there is no mention of Rosicrucianism in the manuscript. Howe evidently assumes that there is a precise meaning to the term "Rosicrucian," when in fact, the term is nebulous and could be applied to nearly any magical manuscript, regardless of source or date.

The main weakness in Howe's argument is the unimpressive nature of the cipher manuscript itself. Had Westcott or Mathers wanted to forge something, they were both familiar enough with various Cabalistic works and medieval grimoires to come up with something more exciting than the ritual outlines in the cipher manuscript. Had they truly wanted to deceive, they could have forged a letter and charter from Christian Rosencruz, Elias Ashmole, or even Doctor Dee.

---

* Meaning that it belonged to the (possibly) mythical sect of magicians said to have been in existence in the sixteenth and seventeenth centuries.

After dealing with the cipher manuscript, Howe proceeds to analyze the letters from Germany. He had these letters examined by an
graphological expert who concluded that "no one born and educated
in Germany would have written such jargon," and that the text was
full of "anglicisms which no German would have used." From this
Howe concludes that Westcott forged the letters and that their source,
Fraulein Sprengel, didn't exist.

There is at least one alternative that Howe ignores: Fraulein Sprengel might have been born in England and moved to Germany as a
young child. She might have never learned to write in English, but
still have used anglicisms in her German. This notion would seem to
be reinforced by the fact that her close associates in Germany were
British. While it may be true that orthographic and grammatical
errors abound, it doesn't necessarily follow that they're the result of an
Englishman's attempted forgery. They could just as easily be the result
of simple illiteracy, especially during a time when women's education
was frequently neglected.

Howe then points out that there have been other cases where
occultists have fabricated legendary characters, such as Madame
Blavatsky's spiritual guides. Howe's attempt to create guilt by comparison remains unconvincing. The fact that other occultists have created
imaginary characters doesn't prove that Westcott was doing the same.

Howe misses the most important objection to Westcott's having
fabricated Fraulein Sprengel. Westcott was recruiting for the Golden
Dawn from Masonic friends. If he were trying to impress them with a
legendary source, why fabricate a woman? After all, Freemasonry is a
primarily male phenomenon. Most men in the Victorian era were
horrified at the very notion of women *voting*. They must have reacted
with some alarm to the notion that the Golden Dawn's authority
rested on communications from a female. If Westcott were trying to

deceive, surely he would have had enough intelligence to fabricate a male magus to confer his lodge's authority.

Throughout the chapter, Howe seems determined to paint everyone involved as negatively as possible. It is true that the Golden Dawn suffered from a certain amount of posturing, self-promotion and internal conflict. It is also true that there were accusations and counter-accusations of various improprieties. However, this kind of behavior is par for the course in religious or quasi-religious organizations. The founding members of the Golden Dawn were human beings and thus had very real human failings.

This brings us to what is most troubling about Howe's analysis. It is clear throughout Howe's work that he lacks a fundamental respect for his subject matter. He is always ready to make a snide remark about "occultists." For example, Howe states that "occultists are not the most skeptical of mortals," and "occultists…are liable to confuse illusion and reality." It is almost as if Howe needs to feel superior, and worse, to point out his superiority at every opportunity. This is not the attitude of a serious researcher; it is the attitude of a tabloid journalist.

Howe doesn't even bother to be consistent. He quotes A.E. Waite extensively and with evident approval, even though Waite was just as much an occultist as Mathers and Westcott. Howe's criticism of occultists is both prejudiced and absurd. Religious beliefs, however unusual, do not disqualify someone from exercising sound scholarship, nor do they automatically render one a forger. For example, many of the great biblical scholars have been Jesuits. Few people criticize their biblical scholarship on the grounds that they have deep religious beliefs.

In short, we really can't take Howe's research into the origins of the Golden Dawn very seriously. He builds his case with a combination of faulty logic, surmise, and guilt by association. He clearly has little respect for his subject matter and is so biased against occultists that his analysis of the evidence is worse than useless. In this regard, it is just as well that Howe isn't being held to the same kind of negative scrutiny that he directs at the Golden Dawn. If I were as uncharitable as Howe, I might conclude that his refusal to reveal the ownership and location of the source documents is simply an attempt to stifle alternative interpretations. By holding a monopoly on his sources, Howe sets himself up to appear every bit as mysterious and evasive as the occultists that he holds in such contempt.

The importance of Golden Dawn is the effect it had in reviving the ancient works of Angel Magic that had been hidden for so long. Between the two of them, Mathers and Westcott delved into this relatively obscure branch of human learning and brought it, as if newly born, into the modern world. They accomplished this with considerable scholarship and translating ability. Westcott's translation of the *Sepher Yetzirah* and his commentaries on the Cabala are both erudite and interesting. Mathers's translations of medieval grimoires like *The Sacred Magic of Abramelin the Mage* and *The Key of Solomon* are nothing short of brilliant.

YEATS AND CROWLEY

Perhaps the most famous member of Golden Dawn was the poet W.B. Yeats who, as result of the training he received from Mathers, may have practiced some sort of Angel Magic with his wife Georgiana Hyde-Lee. Under his tutelage, Georgiana performed automatic writing and speech that provided the raw material for one of Yeats's most famous works, *A Vision*. Yeat's work is an excellent example of something lasting and good resulting from the practice of Angel

Magic. Like the best scrying of Edward Kelly, Yeats' *A Vision* combines philosophy, magic, psychology, history, and autobiography into a set of highly symbolic poems.

If Yeats was the most famous member of the Golden Dawn, the most *infamous* was Aleister Crowley.* Much has been written about Crowley, who played upon post-Victorian predjudices and fears by living a Bohemian life that included heavy doses of magic, sex, and drug addiction. Despite his notoriety, Crowley did much to bring the concept of Angel Magic into the twentieth century.

Crowley saw Angel Magic as a purely practical matter. If it worked, then it didn't matter where it came from. Crowley devoted a great deal of time and effort to codifying and rationalizing the rituals of Angel Magic. He constructed a complex philosophical system that was based as much upon psychology as it was upon historical Angel Magic. Rather than imitating the beliefs and practices of the magicians of the past, he created a new vision for magical practice. Crowley went through the various grimoires, extracting the common elements, and then assigned a psychological meaning to each element. For example, the magical circle symbolized the completeness of the universe, while the magical sword represented the power of the mind to make analytical decisions.

Crowley united the ancient art of Angel Magic with the rapidly developing philosophies of Freudian and Jungian psychology. To Crowley, an Angel Magic ceremony was a mental, emotional and spiritual experiment in which the Magus exalted himself into a peak state where he or she could see, hear, and even smell Angelic beings.[2]

---

* Crowley hated Yeats, who correctly pointed out that Crowley's talents as a poet were, at best, questionable.

The Singing of the Blessed

Angel Magic
Today

ngel Magic is still practiced today in many forms. New Age mediums regularly "channel" Angels to provide advice and guidance to themselves and their friends. Pagans in woodland groves invoke the fairy power of the nature spirits. Catholic priests still perform exorcisms to drive evil spirits from the bodies of possessed parishoners. Underneath the veneer of modern day materialism, the belief in Angel Magic exists virtually unchanged from its origins in the beginning of civilization.

Not surprisingly, there are still Angel Magi who practice the ancient ceremonies of Angel Magic. Several years ago, I had the opportunity to witness an Angel Magic ceremony, performed much in the way they had been performed in the Renaissance. Naturally, I jumped at the chance to observe something which, up until then, had remained a purely scholarly interest.

I have to admit I was excited as I drove the considerable distance to where the Angel Magus lived. I had been spending so much time researching the subject that I had come to think of Angel Magic as something tied to the distant past. The idea that I'd be talking with an actual Angel Magus was more than intriguing.

Of course, in the back of my mind, I really wasn't expecting much. After all, I was in Southern California—a location with a well-deserved reputation for odd people with even odder beliefs. This was a long way from medieval Europe, where the Angel Magi of the past attempted by bold experiment to wrest the secrets of the universe from God's highest servants.

The directions led me to a modest house in one of the older suburbs. Set back from the road and with a high fence around it, there was little to distinguish it from the hundreds of other houses on the crowded streets. Nothing, that is, except for a tasteful wooden sign bearing a word that to me, a scholar of the arcane, meant much, but which would attract no undue attention from the neighbors.

The bell at the gate was answered by a bearded man in casual dress, solidly built, in his late thirties or early forties. As we walked to the house I noticed that there was an economy of movement about him that suggested a military background. We stopped at the doorway and chatted for a moment.

My first impression was that there was nothing particularly unusual about him. He was friendly, but reserved, with a certain distance in his eyes that seemed to say, "I have seen strange things." (I have seen the same expression on the faces of Buddhist monks in the mountains of Southeast Asia.)

We were soon joined by his wife—a shapely, raven-haired woman perhaps half his age. I chuckled to myself, remembering the tales of Merlin and Nimue, the Lady of the Lake. The Magus showed me to his library, where we spent a few minutes comparing and contrasting volumes. He had an excellent grasp of the broad scope of Angel Magic, and was interested in my recent breakthroughs in the dating of the rituals.

Once it was clear that we felt comfortable with each other, I asked if it would be possible for me to witness a ceremony. He told me that he did not usually permit outsiders to attend his experiments, but he would make an exception in my case.

We settled on the couch to await that arrival of the rest of the Magical lodge. As they arrived and sat with us, the conversation picked up slowly, and I began to learn more about the people who were to perform the ceremony. I would have been hard-pressed to imagine a more random group of people. There was a belly dancer, a Ph.D., a pre-med student, a technical writer, a waitress, an accountant, and a programmer. There was little to distinguish them from people you might meet on the street, unless it would be a faint echo of that peculiar "otherworldliness" that I had seen in my host.

"You might wonder," the Magus told me, "Why we use a group of people in our ceremonies. We find that it's easier to build up a head of steam when we get together. It's possible, of course, to practice Angel Magic alone, but it's more difficult to get a manifestation."

I was told that I could not observe the ceremony from outside the circle—"it wouldn't be safe"—so I donned a black robe with the rest of them. We threaded into a room at the back of the house that had been made into a permanent temple, of sorts. The walls were painted black, and around the line of the ceiling were the twelve symbols of the zodiac. There were foot-long reproductions of tarot cards hanging on the walls, and several charts filled with strange letters. In the center of the room was a tall altar with a gigantic crystal ball upon it. It was surrounded by a number of short stools and a wooden circle painted with runes and signs.

The Magus performed the opening ceremony while waving a heavy sword in the air, chanting in stentorian tones that resonated against the bare, blackened walls. Incense coiled up from the alter, filling the room with the rich aroma of a Catholic mass. The Magus sat down and opened a large leather-bound book. It was, as I recall, the invocation from the Lemegeton. From time to time, the Magus would pause, and his wife would strike a tiny bell.

Everyone was staring at the crystal as a palpable air of expectation filled the room. The Magus proceeded to his conjurations, reading the barbaric names with a sense of certainty and urgency. "Why do you delay? Appear before us, or we shall cast your signature into the flame!" Finally, he sat down, his face beaded in sweat. Then he passed the book to the woman on his left, who began the conjuration all over again in a soft and seductive voice. "Appear before us, Angel! You are constrained by the words and talismans that bind you to our will!" Finally, she too became exhausted and handed the book to the next participant.

"It seems to be taking a long time," I remarked to the young man next to me.

"It's usually not this difficult," he told me, "It's harder when there's an outsider present."

They continued to pass the book around, each person conjuring, demanding that the Angel appear in the crystal stone. At one point, I realized that I had become extremely sleepy. The rhythm of the chant was hypnotic, and the smoke hung heavy in the sealed room. I felt myself drooping on my stool and had to force myself to stay awake.

Suddenly, everybody in the room was staring at the youngest woman in the circle. "I see it," she said, staring round-eyed into the crystal. Her hand was trembling where it rested on her knee.

The Magus took back his book and began another conjuration—a binding spell to hold the Angel inside the stone. I peered closely into the crystal, but I saw nothing. Whatever it was, apparently it was visible only to the young lady. The other participants weren't even looking at the stone; instead, they were watching the young woman carefully. One of them pulled out a pen and notebook.

The Magus took the young woman's hand as if to steady her nerves. "He's doing that so he can make sure she doesn't get carried too deeply into that trance," the man beside me whispered. The Magus continued with his conjurations and the young lady's body became less tense. At last she spoke, "The Angel will answer your questions."

Everyone except myself, it seemed, had come into the circle with a particular question that they wanted answered. The Angel that they had conjured was sacred to Venus, so the questions were about love and relationships. The answers seemed ambiguous, at least to me. Perhaps I knew too little about my companions to understand the context.

When it came time for me to ask my question, I was at a bit of a loss. Without really thinking about it, I asked if I would ever fall completely and utterly in love, an event that had yet to happen to me. I received an answer, but it meant little to me at the time.

As the questioning moved around the circle, something in the atmosphere of the room seemed to change. The black robes, which were really nothing more than opaque, shapeless bags, seemed like clinging lingerie. I felt a powerful, almost irresistible attraction to the young lady who was gazing into the stone.

"Stop it!" The Magus' voice cut through the heavy air. I thought for a moment that he was talking to me, but his command was clearly directed at the crystal. The Magus took his sword and held it between the crystal and the young woman. "You are to stay inside the stone!"

he said, "You shall not invade her body." The young woman slumped off her seat into a faint and the sexual energy in the room disappeared as suddenly as it had appeared.

The Magus took up his book and read the dismissal. Somebody threw open a window. I felt sweaty as if drenched in tepid water. The fresh air was crisp with the scent of the Eucalyptus trees outside. The young lady on the floor shook herself awake and reseated herself. The Magus closed the circle with another Pentagram ritual and the ceremony was over.

"A not altogether unsuccessful experiment," the Magus told me afterwards, "We did make contact and we did receive some knowledge. Whether it proves useful or not, I suppose that only time will tell." He seemed quietly pleased.

"What was all that 'not invading the body'?" I asked.

"Ah, that!" He laughed. "These things happen. Angels—even surprisingly exalted ones—are intensely curious about the material world and crave to experience it directly. Sometimes they take over human bodies, in which case they're capable of accomplishing amazing acts—sometimes to the benefit of mankind, sometimes not—it all depends upon the nature of the Angel. The Angels of Mercury, for example, are notoriously capable of vast mischief. The young lady had once been possessed by a Venusian Angel during a previous experiment. The Magus she was working with neglected to dismiss the Angel out of her body. The results were perhaps predictable: She almost immediately became pregnant." There was a twinkle in his eye that made me wonder if I was supposed to take the story seriously. "She didn't want a repeat performance," he continued, "so I stopped the ceremony and dismissed the Angel as soon as it tried to possess her body."

"Did you know for certain that she would be the one to see the Angel in the stone?"

The Magus fingered his beard, considering. "She was the most likely, because she has a natural affinity in her astrological chart to the planet Venus. If we had been working a different kind of Angel, it probably would have been somebody else. I myself often see Jupiterian Angels when we conjure them. However, I consider that more a nuisance than anything else. After all, somebody has to keep the train on the tracks!"

I tried to press him for more information, but he pleaded that he was tired. As I drove home, I wondered what Doctor Dee would have thought of the entire experience. To tell the truth, I wasn't certain what I thought of it myself.

FROM THE REVELATION OF ST. JOHN

Appendix

Angel Magic Signatures, Seals and Alphabets

This appendix provides a key to understanding, translating and identifying the source of nearly any medieval grimoire. It also provides source material for anyone wishing to create Angelic talismans. Angelic talismans are objects—usually pieces of jewelry—into which Angels invest their power. A talisman thus "charged" is said to carry the same energy as the Angel. For example, a talisman inscribed with the signatures of Mars might help a martial artist compete at a tournament.

Planetary Signatures

These signatures probably contain the names of angels coded into magical alphabets and ciphers. Due to repeated copying from manuscript to manuscript, it is no longer possible to decipher much of the original names, even with a complete collection of magical alphabets. The individual lines shown in Figure 23 come from a variety of sources:

Line 1 is from an ancient Arabic manuscript.[1]

Lines 2 through 4 are from an unpublished manuscript attributed to Cardanus.[2]

Lines 5 through 7 are from a work attributed to Trithemeus.[3]

Line 8 is from an unpublished sixteenth century Latin manuscript.[4]

Line 9 is from the *Heptameron*.[5]

Line 10 is from the French *Key of Solomon*.[6]

Line 11 is from Agrippa.[7]

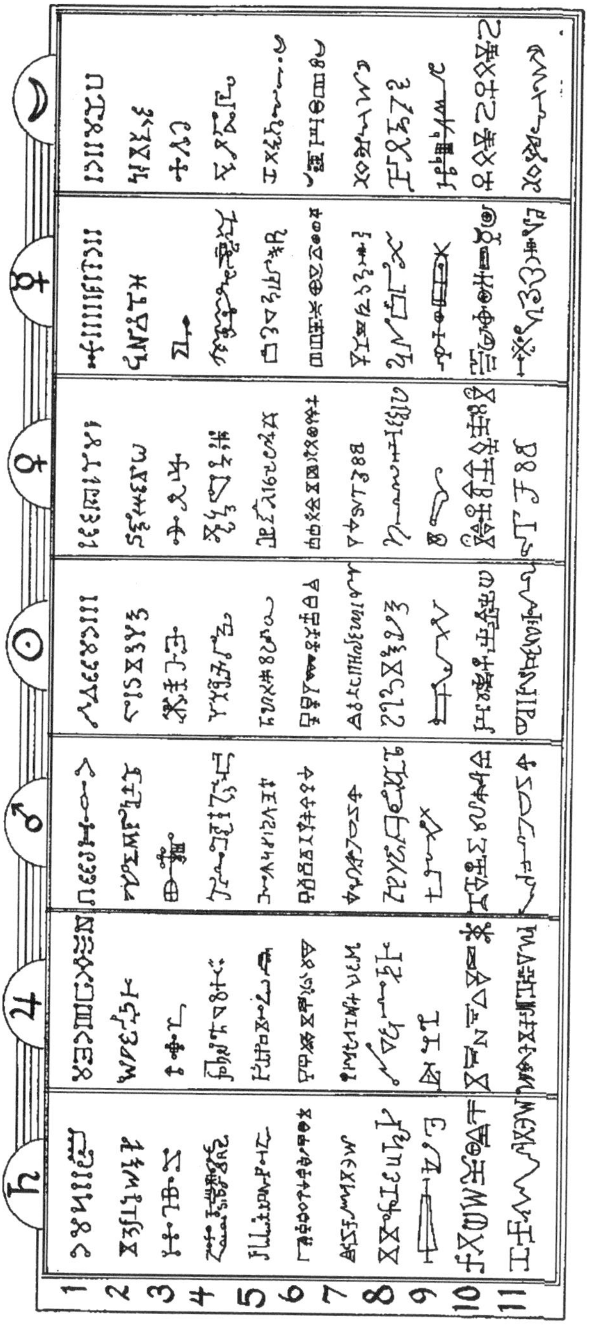

FIGURE 23. PLANETARY SIGNATURES

SEALS OF THE PLANETARY ANGELS

These seals are from an unpublished Greek manuscript. They appear to be monogram talismans constructed from Angelic names transcribed into Angel Magic alphabets such as those given in Figures 32 and 35.

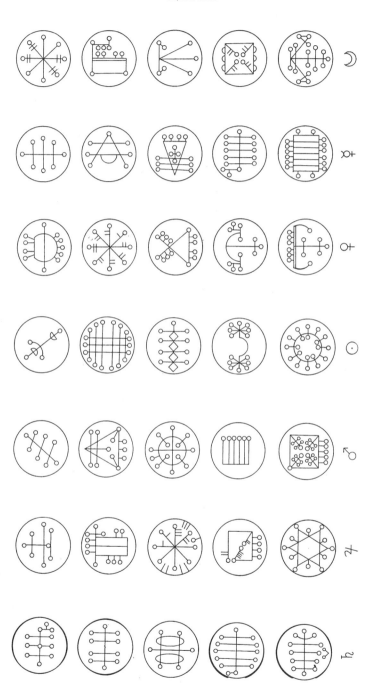

FIGURE 24. PLANETARY SEALS

MAGICAL SQUARES OF THE PLANETS

These are the planetary tables given by the renaissance magician Cornelius Agrippa. Each table is supposed to be sacred to a particular planet and thus able to control the angels whose characters are aligned with that planetary influence.[8]

4	9	2
3	5	7
8	1	6

FIGURE 25. SQUARE OF SATURN

4	14	15	1
9	7	6	12
5	11	10	8
16	2	3	13

FIGURE 26. SQUARE OF JUPITER

11	24	7	20	3
4	12	25	8	16
17	5	13	21	9
10	18	1	14	22
23	6	19	2	15

FIGURE 27. SQUARE OF MARS

6	32	3	34	35	1
7	11	27	28	8	30
19	14	16	15	23	24
18	20	22	21	17	13
25	29	10	9	26	12
36	5	33	4	2	31

FIGURE 28. SQUARE OF SOL

22	47	16	41	10	35	4
5	23	43	17	42	11	29
30	6	24	49	18	36	12
13	31	7	25	43	19	37
38	14	32	1	26	44	20
21	39	8	33	2	27	45
46	15	40	9	34	3	28

FIGURE 29. SQUARE OF VENUS

8	58	59	3	4	62	63	1
49	15	14	52	53	11	10	56
41	23	22	44	45	19	18	48
32	34	35	29	28	38	39	25
40	26	27	37	36	30	31	33
17	47	46	20	21	43	42	24
9	35	54	12	13	51	50	16
64	2	3	61	60	6	7	57

FIGURE 30. SQUARE OF MERCURY

37	78	29	70	21	62	13	54	5
6	38	79	30	71	22	63	14	46
47	7	39	80	31	72	23	55	15
16	48	8	40	81	32	64	24	56
57	17	49	9	41	73	33	65	25
26	58	18	50	1	42	74	34	66
67	27	59	10	51	2	43	75	35
36	68	19	60	11	52	3	44	76
77	28	69	20	61	12	53	4	45

FIGURE 31. SQUARE OF THE MOON

ANGEL MAGIC ALPHABETS

The alphabets and characters that follow are taken from diverse sources. In some cases, the letters had to be reconstructed where a page had been torn or destroyed by time. These alphabets may be used to translate magical names on talismans, or can be used by the practicing magician to encode new talismans. Note that the numbers along the top are used to identify the alphabet, while the numbers in columns (when given) represent the numerical values of the various letters.

Figure 32 represents a set of interrelated Hebraic magical ciphers taken from European magical texts. In some cases they may represent degenerate forms of Hebrew rather than intentional cipher codes.

1. The Characters of Celestial Writing[9]

2. Untitled Hebraic Script[10]

3 "Passing the River"[11]

4. The Malachim[12]

5. Untitled[13]

6. Untitled[14]

7. Untitled[15]

8 Untitled[16]

9. Untitled[17]

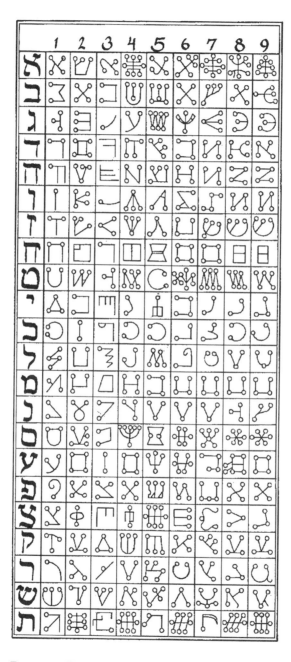

FIGURE 32. EUROPEAN HEBRAIC MAGICAL ALPHABETS

Figure 33 represents a set of ancient Semitic alphabets that are related to the magical scripts given in Figure 32. All of these alphabets are from the same source.[18]

10. Hieroglyphics

11. Hieractic

12. Demotic

13. Ancient Phoenician

14. Numidian

15. Early Hebrew

16. Aramaic

17. Estrangelo

18. Palmyrean

19. Kufic

FIGURE 33. SEMITIC MAGICAL ALPHABETS

Figure 34 presents a set of miscellaneous Hebraic scripts that appeared in Europe. Alphabets 22 and 23 are actually of Middle Eastern origin and are proved to show a contrast with Alphabets 24 and 25.

20. Old Hellenic (pre-Christian)[19]

21. Old Italic (pre-Christian)[20]

22. Samaritan[21]

23. Syrian[22]

24. The Alphabet of the Magi[23]

25. Magical Alphabet (evidently a form of Syrian)[24]

26. Degenerate form of Hebrew found an eleventh century European manuscript.[25]

FIGURE 34. HEBRAIC MAGICAL ALPHABETS

Figure 35 presents a set of Arabic magical alphabets that were used to form the monograph talismans found in magical text such as the Goetia. These alphabets are also related to the alphabets in Figure 23. All are untitled.[26]

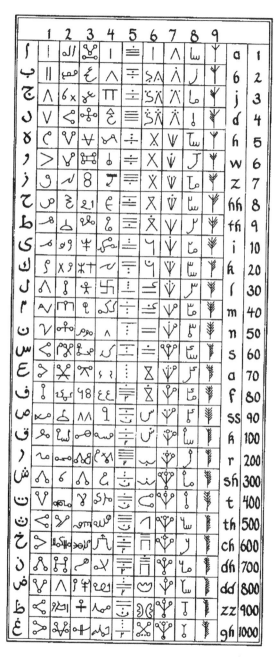

FIGURE 35. ARABIC MAGICAL ALPHABETS

Figure 36 presents a set of Greek ciphers that are possible survivals from traditional Gnostic magical alphabets. All are untitled.[27]

FIGURE 36. GREEK MAGICAL ALPHABETS

Figure 37 gives a set of alphabets that have been adapted to Latin
Script. These alphabets are European in origin and are apparently
unrelated to the other magical alphabets. They may, in some cases,
represent survivals of archaic languages. Note that the Enochian
alphabet does not contain all the possible Latin phonemes.

1. The Theban Alphabet[28]

2. The Enochian Alphabet[29]

3. Germanic Runes[30]

4. Universal Letters of Philosophy and Ethics (eleventh
   century.)[31]

5. Alphabet of Incantations and Divinations[32]

6. Untitled Cipher Code (probably a form of Ogham
   script.)[33]

7. Untitled Cipher Code (also probably a form of Ogham
   script.)[34]

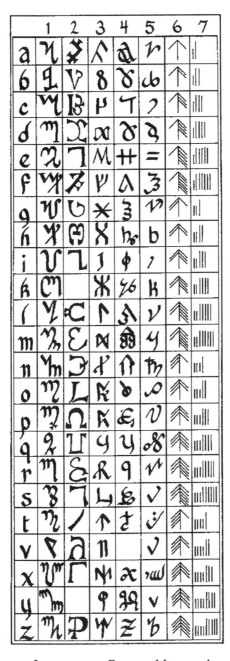

FIGURE 37. LATINATE AND ENGLISH MAGICAL ALPHABETS

HELIODORUS CAST DOWN

Notes

Chapter 1. Introduction to Angel Magic

1. Nancy Gibb. "Angels Among Us," *Time*, December 27, 1993.

2. An excellent account of this is found in the recorded lectures of Joseph Campbell entitled, "Transformation of Myth Through Time." Volume III. (St. Paul: Highbridge Publications).

3. See Carl Jung. *The Basic Writings of C. G. Jung.* (New York: Modern Library, 1959), 37-96.

4. *Strange Stories, Amazing Facts.* (New York: Readers Digest, 1976), 376. According to another story, the visions were reported only after a fictional piece by Arthur Machen was published.

5. Sir James George Frazer, *The Golden Bough.* (New York: Macmillan, 1923), III:11.

6. (Traditional attribution) Cornelius Agrippa, *The Fourth Book of the Occult Philosophy.* (Sine Loco, 1565), 1.

7. See Frazer, *The Golden Bough* for details on these and other examples.

8. Reginald Scot, *The Discoverie of Witchcraft*, (New York: Dover Publications, 1972), 240.

9. This is slightly edited from Marmaduke Pickthall, trans., *The Koran*. (Government Central, Hyderabad-Decca, 1938). In the text, it's unclear whether God or Adam speaks the sentence beginning "Did I not tell you...." I have chosen the magical interpretation, which gives Adam power over the Angels.

10. Scot, 243.

◠⌣

CHAPTER 2. THE SOURCE OF ANGEL MAGIC

1. Paracelsus, *The Archidoxes of Magic*. (London: Askin, 1975), 36.

2. S. Liddell MacGregor Mathers, *The Key of Solomon the King*. (New York: Weiser, 1972), vii.

3. Arthur Edward Waite, *The Book of Ceremonial Magic*. (New York: University, 1961), 9.

4. Francois Lenormant, *Chaldean Magic*. (London: Bagster, 1877), 17.

5. From Schaff, *A Dictionary of the Bible* (Philadelphia: American Sunday School, 1880).

6. E. A. Wallis Budge, *The Gods of the Egyptians*, vol. 1. (New York: Dover, 1969), 3.

7. Ibid., 216.

8. Ibid., 60.

9. Ibid., 216.

10. *The Jerusalem Bible* (New York: Doubleday, 1966), 1032.

11. Mathers, *Key of Solomon,* 96.

12. Ibid., 26.

13. Ibid., 92.

14. See Henry Ansgar Kelly, *The Devil, Demonology and Witchcraft* (New York: Doubleday, 1968), 70.

15. M. Gaster, *The Sword of Moses.* (New York: Weiser, 1973), 37.

16. Ibid., 30.

17. I Samuel, 28:8.

18. Gaster, 1.

19. Ibid., 28.

20. Mathers, *Key of Solomon,* 89.

21. Gaster, 37.

22. See I Samuel, 16:14.

23. Gaster, 15.

24. Aleister Crowley, trans., *Goetia.* (Chicago: DeLaurence, 1916), 52.

25. Mathers, *Key of Solomon,* 67.

26. Mathers, trans., *The Book of the Sacred Magic of Abramelin the Mage.* (New York: Dover, 1975), 216.

27. Manly P. Hall, *The Secret Teachings of All Ages.* (Los Angeles: Philosophical Research Society, 1975), 21-32.

28. *The Jerusalem Bible, New Testament.* (New York: Doubleday, 1966), 234.

29. G. R. S. Mead, *Fragments of a Faith Forgotten.* (New York: University, 1960), 563.

30. Montague Summers, *The Geography of Witchcraft.* (New Jersey: Citadel, 1973), 8.

31. Miniature from the *Bible of St. Paul,* reproduced from *Lost Books of the Bible and the Forgotten Books of Eden* (New York: Lewis Copeland Co.: 1930).

32. Clemens Romanus, *Recognitiones,* Lib. II, cap. 9. Anastasius Sinaita Quæstiones, Quæstio 20.

33. Hall, xxi.

34. Budge, *Gods of the Egyptians,* 178.

35. From a pottery jar in the British Museum.

36. Aleister Crowley, ed. and S.L. MacGregor Mathers, trans., *The Book of Goetia of Solomon the King.* (Inverness: Society for the Propagation of Religious Truth, 1904), illustration facing 38.

37. Ibid., loc. cit.

⤸

Chapter 3. The Survival of Angel Magic

1. William of Malmesbury, Lib. II, c. 10.

2. Codex 1761, Nationalbibliothek Wein, 11th Century.

3. Reproduced from *The Lost Books of the Bible.* (Cleveland: Forum Books, 1963).

4. Gaster, *Sword of Moses,*15-16.

5. See Israel Regardie, *How to Make and Use Talismans.* (New York: Weiser, 1972).

6. Rev. Horace K. Mann, *The Lives of the Popes*, vol. v. (London: Kegan Paul, 1925), 13.

7. Hellmut Ritter, *Picatrix*, German translation of Arabic. (London: Warburg Institute, 1962), foreword. Also see Mathers, *Key of Solomon*, 1.

8. Mann, *Lives of the Popes*, 14-15, 22.

9. William of Malmesbury, Lib. II, c. 10.

10. Naude, *Apoliogie des Grands Hommes Accuses de Magic*. Malmesbury, ubi supra.

11. William of Malmesbury, *De Gestis Regum Anglorum*, vol. 1. (Majesty's Stationary Office, 1887), 203. Also see William Godwin, *The Lives of the Necromancers*. (London: Mason, 1834), 231-234.

12. Summers, *Geography of Witchcraft*, 523.

13. Walter L. Wakefield, *Heresies of the High Middle Ages*. (New York: Columbia University, 1969).

14. Summers, 361.

15. Sloane MSS 2731. British Library.

16. Crowley, trans., *Goetia*, 47-48.

17. Ibid., 57.

18. Scot, *Discoverie of Witchcraft*, 227.

19. Eliphas Levi, *The History of Magic*. (New York: Weiser, 1973), 207-211.

20. From the "Triumph of Death," ascribed to Francesco Traini in the Campo Santo, Pisa.

21. Ibid., loc. cit.

22. Summers, *Geography of Witchcraft*, 256.

23. James J. Walsh, *The Popes and Science.* (Fordham University, 1971), 129.

24. Naude, *Apoliogie,* cap. 17.

25. *Biographie Universelle.*

26. Codex Vindobonesis 11313, Imperial Library of Vienna. A version of this *Magical Calendar,* attributed to Tycho Brahe, was printed in 1979 by Adam McLean under the auspices of Magnus Opus Hermetic Sourceworks in Edinburgh, Scotland.

27. Paulus Jovius, *Elogia Doctorum Virorum,* c.101

28. Weirus, *De Praestigiis Demonum,* Lib. II, c.v. & 11, 12

29. Francis Coxe, *The Wickedness of the Magicall Sciences.* (London, 1561).

30. Scot, *Discoverie of Witchcraft,* 262.

31. Barnet, ed., *The Genius of the Early English Theatre.* (New York: Mentor, 1962), 109-110.

∽

CHAPTER 4. THE MAKING OF AN ANGEL MAGUS

1. A number of passages in this chapter are taken, with some editing, from Godwin's *Lives of the Necromancers,* an interesting book published in 1834 and out of print ever since.

2. See Aleen G. Debus, ed., *John Dee: The Mathematical Praeface to the Elements of Geometrie of Euclid of Megara (1570).* (New York: Science History Publications,1975).

3. From the frontispiece of Meric Casaubon, *A True and Faithful Relation.* (London: Askin, 1974).

4. From Sloane MSS 3188.

5. Sloane MSS 3677, 23. This is Ashmole's much more readable copy of Sloane MSS 3188.

6. Elias Ashmole, *Theatrum Chemicum Britannicum.* (London, 1652), 481.

༺

CHAPTER 5. THE ANGELIC KEYS

1. Casaubon, *True and Faithful Relation*, 73.

2. Mathers, *Key of Solomon*, 51.

3. From Sloane MSS 3191.

4. Ibid.

5. For more information see Donald Laycock, *The Complete Enochian Dictionary.* (London: Askin, 1978).

6. Frances Yates, *Gordiano Bruno and the Hermetic Tradition.* (London: Routledge and Kegan Paul, 1964), 149.

7. Waite, ed., *The Alchemical Writing of Edward Kelly.* (New York: Weiser; 1973), liii.

8. Geoffrey James, "The Key of the Thirty Aires," *The Enochian Magick of Doctor John Dee.* (St. Paul: Llewellyn, 1994), 100.

9. Ibid., 68.

10. Peter French, *John Dee: The World of an Elizabethan Magus.* (London: Routledge & Kegan Paul, 1972), 114.

11. Casaubon, *True and Faithful Relation*, 382.

12. Ibid., 116.

13. Ibid.

14. Regardie, *The Golden Dawn,* vol. iv. (St. Paul: Llewellyn, 1971), 268.

15. Scot, *Discoverie of Witchcraft.*

16. *Funk and Wagnalls Encyclopedia,* vol. 15. Article on Krakow.

17. Casaubon, *True and Faithful Relation,* 158.

18. See "The Secrets of Enoch," *The Lost Books of the Bible.* (Cleveland: Forum Books, 1963), passim.

19. Mead, *Fragments,* 462.

20. Ibid., 188.

21. Ibid., 487.

22. Ibid., 528, 541.

23. Casaubon, *True and Faithful Relation,* 88.

24. Mead, 471.

25. Ibid., 516.

26. Casaubon, 77.

27. Mead, 523.

28. Laycock, *Complete Enochian Dictionary,* 38.

29. Jean Paul Richter, trans., *The Notebooks of Leonardo Da Vinci,* vol. ii. (New York: Dover, 1970), 307.

Chapter 6. The Result of Dee's Magic

1. Casaubon, 229-230.

2. From the frontispiece of Casaubon.

3. Casaubon, 280.

4. Ibid., 25.

5. Ibid.

6. Ibid., 19.

7. Scot, *Discoverie of Witchcraft*, 183.

8. Godwin, *Necromancers*, 380.

9. Waite, *Alchemical Writings*, 6.

10. Waite, *Alchemists Through The Ages*. (New York: Steiner, 1970), 158.

11. Article on Marlowe, *American Heritage Encyclopedia*. Retrieved from CompuServe.

12. French, *John Dee*, 171.

13. Yates, *The Occult Philosophy in the Elizabethan Age*. (London: Routledge and Kegan Paul), 116.

14. Barnet, *Early English Theatre*. I've done a little editing to make the passage understandable to the average reader.

15. From Dee's preface to Sloane MSS 3188.

16. Yates, *Occult Philosophy*, 120.

17. *The Complete Plays and Poems of William Shakespeare*. (Cambridge: Houghton Mifflin: 1942), 565.

CHAPTER 7. FAIRY MAGIC

1. Sloane MSS 1727, London: British Museum, 17th Century. As quoted in Katherine Briggs, *An Encyclopedia of Fairies.* (New York: Pantheon, 1976), 378.

2. From Richard Bovet's *Pandaemonium or the Devil's Cloyster,* 1684. Reproduced by Katharine Briggs in *An Encyclopedia of Fairies,* 35.

3. Sloane.

4. Ashmole MSS 1406, Oxford: Bodleian Library, 17th Century. As quoted in Briggs, 376.

5. Ibid., loc. cit.

6. Ibid., 377.

7. Scot, *Discoverie of Witchcraft,* 234.

8. Ibid., loc. cit.

9. Sir Walter Scott, *Demonology and Witchcraft.* (London: Murray, 1830).

10. Robert Rirk, *The Secret Commonwealth of Elves, Fauns and Fairies.* (Mackay Stirling, 1691). As quoted in Briggs, Encyclopedia, 351.

11. Ibid., loc. cit.

12. John Gregorson Campbell, *Witchcraft and Second Sight in the Highlands and Islands of Scotland.* (Glasgow: MacLehose, 1902), 180.

⤳

Chapter 8. Angel Magic and the Golden Dawn

1. Ellic Howe, *The Magicians of the Golden Dawn*. (New York: Weiser, 1972), Chapter 1.

2. See Aleister Crowley, *Magic Without Tears*. (St. Paul: Llewellyn, 1973), 362.

⤳

Appendix

1. Pseudo-Magriti, *The Gold of the Sages*, trans. Ritter. (Warburg Institute, 1968).

2. Cardanus, *De Rerum Varietate*, Lib. XVI. (Basileae, 1557).

3. Trithemeus, *Calandarium Magicum Naturale*. Codex 11313, Nationalbibliothek Wein, 1503.

4. *Liber Imaginum Lunae*. Biblioteca Nazionale Firenze, 15th century.

5. Peter d' Apono, *Eptameron, Elementa Magica*. (Sine Loco, 1565).

6. *Clavicules de Salomon*. Landsdowne 1203, 17th century.

7. Agrippa, *De Occulta Philosophia*. (Sine Loco, 1533), as presented in Barrett, Frances, *The Magus*. (New York: University Books: 1967), facing second page 64.

8. See Regardie, *How to Make and Use Talismans*.

9. Barrett, loc. cit.

10. Codex Philos. graec. 108, 17th century.

11. Barrett, loc. cit.

12. Ibid., loc. cit.

13. Bartolozzi, *Inhumati Bebiltecha Magna Rabbinica.* (Rome, 1675).

14. Ibid.

15. Ibid.

16. Ibid.

17. Ibid.

18. Ballhorn, *Grammatography.* (1861)

19. Ibid.

20. Ibid.

21. Ibid.

22. Ibid.

23. Paul Christian, *The History and Practice of Magic.* (Secaucus: Citadel Press, 1969), 147.

24. Barrett, loc. cit.

25. Codex 1761, Nationalbibliothek Wein, 11th century.

26. Ballhorn, *Grammatography.* (1861).

27. Codex Philos. graec. 108, 17th century.

28. Barrett, loc. cit.

29. See James, *Enochian Magick,* for an alternate version of this script.

30. Codex 1761, Nationalbibliotek Wein, 11th century.

31. Ibid.

32. Ibid.

33. Ibid.

34. Ibid.

Suggested Reading

In this list of suggested reading, I've omitted manuscripts and rare books that would be inaccessible to the normal reader. Most of the books in this list have been published within the last thirty years and should be available to those who make a really diligent search.

GRIMOIRES

The Sixth and Seventh Books of Moses. Minneapolis: Tau Universal Publishing Co. A collection of spurious conjurations and late Victorian restorations of ancient texts. Suitable only for adolescents.

Raphael's Ancient Manuscript of Talismanic Magic. Chicago: de Laurence Co., 1916. A handwritten version of various Agrippan sources available elsewhere.

Barrett, Francis, ed. *The Magus*. New York: University Books,1967. A collection of fragments from Agrippa's Occult Philosophy, (including "book four"), the Heptameron and some other sources. Interesting only as a curio as other, more accurate editions of these works are available.

Crowley, Aleister, ed. *Goetia*. Letchworth: Garden City Press, 1976. Actually translated by S. L. MacGregor Mathers and published by Crowley, who attributed it (rather meanly) to a "dead hand." This is the first book of the Lemegeton, the rest of which remains to be published.

Driscoll, Daniel, trans. *The Sworn Book of Honorius the Magician*. New Jersey: Heptangle, 1977. A very beautiful handset volume, now quite rare. Probably one of the earliest European manuscripts, this contains a seven-pointed talisman that's clearly the root of the seven-pointed "Sigil of Aemeth" that figures so largely in Dee's magical system. An interesting text in every way.

Gaster, M., trans. *The Sword of Moses*. New York: Weiser, 1973. A classic. The key to understanding the dating of the medieval grimoires, this shows ceremonial magic in a very early form.

Hay, George, ed. *The Necronomicon*. New Jersey: Neville Spearman, 1978. An elaborate hoax proving that some people have a great deal too much time on their hands.

James, Geoffrey, trans. *The Enochian Magick of Doctor John Dee*. St. Paul: Llewellyn, 1984. It's been called the definitive version of Dee's magical manuscripts (even by people other than me.)

MacGregor Mathers, S. L., trans. *The Sacred Magic of Abramelin the Mage*. Chicago: de Laurence Co., 1948. An interesting classic that's connected with the Golden Dawn tradition. Reputed to be a very difficult and dangerous set of rituals to perform.

————. *The Key of Solomon the King.* New York: Weiser, 1972. The classic grimoire, with elements that probably date from several centuries B.C. A definitive text, especially important in comparison with the Sword of Moses.

————. *The Grimoire of Armadel.* New York: Weiser, 1980. Another classic text presented courtesy of the indefatigable Mathers. Contains a number of particularly interesting sigils.

Machus, Marius. *The Secret Grimoire of Turiel.* London: The Aquarian Press, 1971. A late version of the Arbatel.

Turner, Robert, ed. *Arbatel.* New Jersey: Heptangle, 1979. A very simple and straightforward grimoire. Another beautiful and rare book from the hand of Daniel Driscoll.

Turner, Robert, trans. *The Fourth Book of Occult Philosophy.* London: Askin, 1978. A reproduction of a collection of magical texts published in 1655. The existence of the original shows the continuing popularity of Angel Magic.

————. *Of Occult Philosophy Book Four: Magical Ceremonies.* New Jersey: Heptangle, 1985. A more readable transcription than the Askin facsimile. Another beautiful letterpress book, this has now become quite rare.

Scot, Reginald. *The Discoverie of Witchcraft.* New York: Dover, 1972. Contains a complete manual of Fairy Magic. Extremely interesting for its descriptions of stage magic and the frauds perpetrated by witch trial judges.

Tyson, Donald, ed. *Three Books of the Occult Philosophy.* St. Paul: Llewellyn, 1993. A welcome re-publication of the classic Agrippan text.

Waite, A. E. *The Book of Ceremonial Magic*. New York: University Books, 1961. A classic collection of various texts, interesting because it includes some of the black magical texts that circulated in the eighteenth century. Waite's opinions on dating the manuscripts can be judiciously ignored. Contains fragments of the *Lemegeton*.

ᑍᐦ

"How To" Books

Bardon, Franz. *The Practice of Magical Evocation*. Germany: Dieter Ruggeberg, 1970. A completely different approach from the English and American material. Very original and curious.

Crowley, Aleister. *777*. New York: Weiser, 1970. A collection of correspondences for building congruent magical ceremonies.

———. *Magick Without Tears*. St. Paul: Llewellyn, 1973. A series of letters explaining various aspects of magical practice.

———. *Magick*. New York: Weiser, 1976. As maddening and obscure as it is informative, Crowley's work continues to fascinate. The definitive modern work on Angel Magic—if you can tolerate the author's insufferable arrogance.

Davidson, Gustav. *A Dictionary of Angels*. New York: Macmillian, 1967. Recently reissued in paperback, this interesting collection includes (very democratically) fallen as well as heavenly Angels.

Godwin, David. *Godwin's Cabalistic Encyclopedia*. St. Paul: Llewellyn, 1994. The classic reference work. Don't leave the physical plane without it.

Gray, William. *Magical Ritual Methods*. London: Helios, 1971. An somewhat heavily-written text but full of excellent advice.

Kraig, Donald Michael. *Modern Magick*. St. Paul: Llewellyn, 1994. Explains how to evoke entities to physical appearance and how to use the Greater and Lesser Keys of Solomon.

Laycock, Donald. *The Complete Enochian Dictionary*. London: Askin, 1978. The definitive reference source for the Angelical language.

Schueler, Gerald and Betty Schueler. *Enochian Magic: A Practical Manual*. St. Paul: Llewellyn, 1993. A manual for the beginner and seasoned magician alike. The Schuelers are among the most prolific Enochian researchers alive today.

Tyson, Donald. *How to Make and Use a Magic Mirror*. St. Paul: Llewellyn, 1990. Step-by-step instructions with a historical perspective on mirror lore in magic and literature.

———. *The New Magus: The Modern Magician's Practical Guide*. St. Paul: Llewellyn, 1988. A practical framework for a personal system of magic.

———. *Ritual Magic: What It Is & How To Do It*. St. Paul: Llewellyn, 1992. An overview of the choices and philosophies of modern magical practice.

———. *An Advanced Guide to Enochian Magick*. St. Paul: Llewellyn. Included are exercises, complete rituals, and outlines for multi-level magical operations.

Vinci, Leo. *Gmicalzoma: An Enochian Dictionary*. London: Regency, 1976. An interesting book, but superceded by Laycock's work.

∾

HISTORICAL BACKGROUND

Ayton, William Alexander. *The Life of John Dee*. London: First Impressions, 1992. A particularly interesting biography that also tells the story about Dee's son Arthur.

Clulee, Nicholas H. *John Dee's Natural Philosophy: Between Science and Religion*. London: Routledge, 1988. A definitive study of Dee's philosophical life. Absolutely first rate. A classic.

Dee, John. *The Mathematical Praeface to the Elements of Geometrie of Euclid of Megara*. New York: Science History Publications, 1975. The book that established Dee's fame prior to his Angel Magic experiments.

———. *The Hieroglyphic Monad*. New York: Weiser. 1975. A curious and impenetrable work that's puzzled whomever has examined it.

French, Peter J. *John Dee: The World of an Elizabethan Magus*. London: Routledge & Kegan Paul, 1972. Still the definitive biography of Dee, albeit one that doesn't follow any chronological order.

Laurence, Richard, trans. *The Book of Enoch The Prophet*. Minneapolis: Wizards Bookshelf, 1976. An interesting contrast to Dee's Enochian material.

Mead, G. R. S. *Pistis Sophia*. New Jersey: University, 1974. A Gnostic miscellany collected from various sources. Interesting as a study of Gnostic beliefs.

———. *Fragments of a Faith Forgotten*. New York: University. 1960. More Gnostic fragments with extensive commentary. Waite, A. E. The Alchemical Writings of Edward Kelly. New York: Weiser, 1970. An interesting collection of Kelly's work after his sojourn with Dee.

Orchard, James Halliwell. *The Private Diary of Dr. John Dee.* London: AMS Press, 1968. An interesting perspective into Dee's home life and political situation. These are casual references written as marginalia.

Suster, Gerald. *John Dee: Essential Readings.* London: Crucible, 1986. An interesting selection of John Dee's work in various fields.

Yates, Frances A. *The Rosicrucian Enlightenment.* Boulder: Shambhala, 1978. An insightful view of the development of Magic after Dee.

————. *Giordiano Bruno and the Hermetic Tradition.* London: Routledge & Kegan Paul. 1964. An excellent overview of a Renaissance Angel Magus who forms an interesting contrast with John Dee.

————. *The Occult Philosophy in the Elizabethan Age.* London: Ark Paperbacks. 1983. An essential work for anyone studying the history of Angel Magic and related subjects during the Renaissance.

Index

Buddhism, 4
Cabala, 15-16, 18-19, 31, 33, 85, 98, 101, 142
Caermarthen, 45
Call of the Thirty Aires, 94
Cambridge, 67-68, 115
Cardinal Beno, 51
Celtic runes, 47
ceremonial magic, 24, 91-92, 138, 176
Chaldean Angel Magic, 25
Chaldeans, 32, 43
channeling, 12, 20
charlatan, 12, 75, 97
Cherubim, 3, 128
Christian church, 2-3, 23, 37
Christian dogma, 37
Christian tradition, 2, 50
Christopher Marlowe, 62, 115-116
church, 2-3, 14, 23, 36-38, 40, 43, 45-46, 51, 54-57, 67, 69, 118
collective unconscious, 5
Conjuration, 17, 32, 54, 82-83, 127, 130-131, 148-149
Consecration, 17, 62
contact experiences, 11
Conversation, 17, 73, 147
Count Albert Lasky of Poland, 66, 77-79, 97, 101-103, 106
Count Dracula, 107
Count Rosenburg of Trebona, 66, 107

Cracow, 77-78, 81, 93, 96, 106
crown, 31, 51
crystal, 20, 73, 77, 111, 124, 147-149
crystal sphere, 111
Curtzius, 102, 105
daimon, 3
Daimones, 3
De Occulta Philosphia, 61-63, 76, 135, 185
Dismissal, 17, 150
Divas, 3
divine energy, 4, 12-13, 18, 20
divine names, 17-18, 20, 26, 43, 82
Doctor Faustus, 62-63, 116-118
Donald Laycock, 86, 181
Dr. Wynn Westcott, 137-142
dreams, 6-7, 10-11, 13
druids, 4
Eastern Europe, 93
Edward Talbot, 74
Egyptian Angel Magic, 25, 27-29
Elias Ashmole, 74, 133-134, 139, 181, 184
Eliphas Levi, 139, 179
Elizabeth, 66, 69-71, 77-78, 107, 112, 115-116, 118-119
Ellic Howe, 137, 185
Elohim, 15
Emanuel Swedenborg, 134-135
Emperor Maximilian, 59
Emperor Rudolph, 107, 114

energy source, 12
Enochian, 77, 79, 82, 85-86, 89, 92-94, 96, 172, 181-182, 186
Episcopal churches, 47
Erasmus, 59
Essenes, 36
Euclid, 68-69, 180
excommunication, 56
Fairies, 4, 125, 128-129, 131, 184
Fairy Magic, 121-122, 127, 129-131, 135, 184
folk tales, 1
Francis Barrett, 135
Fraulein Sprengel, 137, 140
Frazer, 13, 175
Freudian, 143
Gabriel, 15, 91
garments, 31, 84, 110
genius, 13, 180
Gerbert, 50-51
Germany, 102, 107, 137, 140
Glastonbury Abbey, 76
Gnostic, 31, 36-41, 43, 50-51, 55, 94-96, 127, 170
Gnostic sects, 36
Gnosticism, 36, 38, 43, 54
gods, 3-4, 12, 25-27, 38, 62, 176, 178
Greenwich, 77
Gregory VII, 51
grimoires, 14-15, 17-18, 21, 23-26, 29, 31, 33-37, 41-42, 49, 52, 54, 82-85, 92, 134, 138-139, 142-143
hallucinating, 90, 111
Hebrew, 15-16, 31-32, 34-35, 46, 52, 73, 82-83, 85, 98, 101, 162, 164, 166
Hebrew mythology, 34
Henry Cornelus Agrippa, 59-62, 66, 93, 135, 154, 158, 175, 185-186
Henry Percy, 115
Heptameron, 62-63, 85, 154
herbs, 29, 32, 34
Herculaneum, 35
heretical documents, 43
Hinduism, 4
hobgoblins, 129
Holy Grail, 5
holy names, 16, 17, 18, 20, 127
human sacrifices, 54
incantations, 18, 25, 31-34, 37, 60, 74-75, 172
Incense, 17, 20-21, 28-29, 31, 148
Invocations, 62
Ishtar, 3
Islamic Angel Magi, 49
J.R.R. Tolkien, 89
Jacob Boehme, 134
Jane Dee, 105-106
Jesus, 37, 122, 124, 127-128
Jesus' exorcisms, 37
Jewish Mysticism, 31
Jewish sages, 33
Jinn, 3
John Dee, 15, 63, 65-67, 82, 99, 116, 118-119, 121, 180-181, 183
John Donne, 115

☾ REACH FOR THE MOON

Llewellyn publishes hundreds of books on your favorite subjects! To get these exciting books, including the ones on the following pages, check your local bookstore or order them directly from Llewellyn.

ORDER BY PHONE
- Call toll-free within the U.S. and Canada, 1-800-THE MOON
- In Minnesota, call (612) 291-1970
- We accept VISA, MasterCard, and American Express

ORDER BY MAIL
- Send the full price of your order (MN residents add 7% sales tax) in U.S. funds, plus postage & handling to:

  Llewellyn Worldwide
  P.O. Box 64383, Dept. K368-9
  St. Paul, MN 55164–0383, U.S.A.

POSTAGE & HANDLING
(For the U.S., Canada, and Mexico)
- $4.00 for orders $15.00 and under
- $5.00 for orders over $15.00
- No charge for orders over $100.00

We ship UPS in the continental United States. We ship standard mail to P.O. boxes. Orders shipped to Alaska, Hawaii, The Virgin Islands, and Puerto Rico are sent first-class mail. Orders shipped to Canada and Mexico are sent surface mail.

International orders: Airmail—add freight equal to price of each book to the total price of order, plus $5.00 for each non-book item (audio tapes, etc.).

Surface mail—Add $1.00 per item.

Allow 2 weeks for delivery on all orders.
Postage and handling rates subject to change.

DISCOUNTS
We offer a 20% discount to group leaders or agents. You must order a minimum of 5 copies of the same book to get our special quantity price.

FREE CATALOG
Get a free copy of our color catalog, *New Worlds of Mind and Spirit*. Subscribe for just $10.00 in the United States and Canada ($30.00 overseas, airmail). Many bookstores carry *New Worlds*— ask for it!

Visit our web site at www.llewellyn.com for more information.

THE ENOCHIAN MAGICK OF DR. JOHN DEE

The Most Powerful System of Magick in Its Original, Unexpurgated Form
Geoffrey James

(formerly *The Enochian Evocation of Dr. John Dee*)

Dr. John Dee's system of Enochian Magick is among the most powerful in the Western tradition, and it has been enormously influential in the practices of the Order of the Golden Dawn. Though long out-of-print, this book has become an occult classic because it holds all the secrets of Dee's private magical workbooks, just as Dee recorded them in the late 16th century.

This indispensable treasure of Enochian lore offers the only definitive version of the famous Angelical Calls or Keys, conjurations said to summon the angels of the heavenly sphere—as well as all the practical information necessary for the experienced magician to reproduce Dee's occult experiments, with details on how to generate the names of the angels, create Enochian talismans, and set up an Enochian temple. Here readers will find the only available version of Dee's system of planetary and elemental magic, plus other material sure to fascinate a new generation of students of Enochian Magick. Explore the source texts that inspired MacGregor Mathers, Aleister Crowley, Israel Regardie, and a host of others and learn to practice angelic magick!

1–56718–367–0, 6 x 9, 248 pp., illus. $14.95

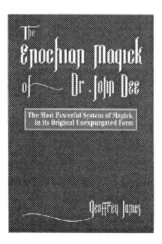

TETRAGRAMMATON
The Secret to Evoking Angelic Powers and the Key to the Apocalypse
Donald Tyson

In Western magick, "Tetragrammaton" is the holiest name of God. It is composed of the four Hebrew letters IHVH and is the occult key that unlocks the meaning behind astrological symbolism, the tarot, the mysteries of the Old Testament and the Book of Revelation, the kabbalah, the Enochian magick of John Dee, and modern ritual magick. It is nothing less than the archetypal blueprint of creation, the basis for such fundamental forms as the DNA double helix and the binary language of modern computers. Its true structure is the great arcanum of occultism, which has never before been explicitly revealed but only hinted at in obscure religious and alchemical emblems. Now, for the first time, its true structure is laid bare in a clear and unambiguous manner, allowing this potent key to open astounding vistas of understanding.

Tetragrammaton is a book for kabbalists, ritual occultists and anyone fascinated by the magic of the Bible. Those seeking proof for the coming of the Apocalypse will be captivated by the justification for Revelation in the Keys.

1-56718-744-7, 320 pp., 7 x 10, softcover $19.95

ENOCHIAN MAGIC
A Practical Manual
Gerald J. Schueler

The powerful system of magic introduced in the 16th century by Dr. John Dee, Astrologer Royal to Queen Elizabeth I, and as practiced by Aleister Crowley and the Hermetic Order of the Golden Dawn, is here presented for the first time in a complete, step-by-step form. There has never before been a book that has made Enochian Magic this easy!

In this book you are led carefully along the path from "A brief history of the Enochian Magical System," through "How to Speak Enochian," "How to Invoke," "The Calls," "Egyptian Deities" and "Chief Hazards" to "How to visit the Aethyrs in Spirit Vision (Astral Projection)." Not a step is missed; not a necessary instruction forgotten.

0–87542–710–3, 288 pp., 5¼ x 8, illus., softcover $9.95

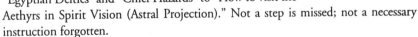

THREE BOOKS OF OCCULT PHILOSOPHY
Completely Annotated, with Modern Commentary—
The Foundation Book of Western Occultism
Henry Cornelius Agrippa, edited and annotated by
Donald Tyson

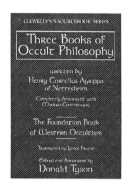

Agrippa's *Three Books of Occult Philosophy* is the single
most important text in the history of Western occultism.
Occultists have drawn upon it for five centuries, although
they rarely give it credit. First published in Latin in 1531
and translated into English in 1651, it has never been
reprinted in its entirety since. Photocopies are hard to
find and very expensive. Now, for the first time in 500 years, *Three Books of Occult
Philosophy* will be presented as Agrippa intended. There were many errors in the
original translation, but occult author Donald Tyson has made the corrections and
has clarified the more obscure material with copious notes.

This is a necessary reference tool not only for all magicians, but also for scholars of the Renaissance, Neoplatonism, the Western Kabbalah, the history of ideas
and sciences and the occult tradition. It is as practical today as it was 500 years ago.
0–87542–832–0, 1,024 pgs., 7 x 10, softcover $39.95

MODERN MAGICK
Eleven Lessons in the High Magickal Arts
Donald Michael Kraig

Modern Magick is the most comprehensive step-by-step
introduction to the art of ceremonial magic ever offered.
The eleven lessons in this book will guide you from the
easiest of rituals and the construction of your magickal
tools through the highest forms of magick: designing your
own rituals and doing pathworking. Along the way you
will learn the secrets of the Kabbalah in a clear and easy-
to-understand manner. You will discover the true secrets of
invocation (channeling) and evocation, and the missing
information that will finally make the ancient grimoires,
such as the "Keys of Solomon," not only comprehensible, but usable. This book also
contains one of the most in-depth chapters on sex magick ever written. *Modern
Magick* is designed so anyone can use it, and it is the perfect guidebook for students
and classes. It will also help to round out the knowledge of long-time practitioners
of the magickal arts.
0–87542–324–8, 592 pgs., 6 x 9, illus., index, softcover $17.95

GODWIN'S CABALISTIC ENCYCLOPEDIA
**Complete Guidance to Both Practical
and Esoteric Applications
David Godwin**

One of the most valuable books on the Cabala is back, with a new and more usable format. This book is a complete guide to Cabalistic magick and gematria in which every demon, angel, power and name of God ... every Sephiroth, Path, and Plane of the Tree of Life ... and each attribute and association is fully described and cross-indexed by the Hebrew, English, and numerical forms.

All entries, which had been scattered throughout the appendices, are now incorporated into one comprehensive dictionary. There are hundreds of new entries and illustrations, making this book even more valuable for Cabalistic pathworking and meditation. It now has many new Hebrew words and names, as well as the terms of Freemasonry, the entities of the Cthulhu mythos, and the Aurum Solis spellings for the names of the demons of the Goetia. It contains authentic Hebrew spellings, and a new introduction that explains the uses of the book for meditation on God names.

The Cabalistic schema is native to the human psyche, and *Godwin's Cabalistic Encyclopedia* will be a valuable reference tool for all Cabalists, magicians, scholars and scientists of all disciplines.

1–56718–324–7, 832 pp., 6 x 9, softcover   **$29.95**

NEW MILLENNIUM MAGICK
**A Complete System of Self-Realization
Donald Tyson**

Magic is not a fossilized art fixed centuries ago by dusty old wizards in foreign lands. To continue as a living, vital discipline, magic must change with the times. We must constantly recreate it using the latest scientific and philosophical techniques.

New Millennium Magic provides a practical framework on which you can base your own personal ritual techniques. By using the universal principles outlined, you can tailor a system of magic to your own background and beliefs. The book clarifies many questions that confront the budding magician in a completely modern way while maintaining traditional and time-honored symbolism and formulae.

Originally published under the title *The New Magus* in 1987, this new edition has been updated and extensively expanded by the author. It contains a wealth of material not included in the original.

If you have found that traditional magic seems musty, illogical, overcomplicated and not appropriate to your lifestyle, *New Millennium Magic* is for you. It will change your ideas of magic forever!

1–56718–745–5, 384 pp., 7 x 10, softcover   **$19.95**